Table Of Contents

PREFACE

As a veteran pastor and missionary Ken Symes understands that true worship of God is foundational for all Christian service and growth. Until one learns to worship God, one cannot understand his true identity and purpose nor find the secret to life itself.

The ancient book of Leviticus holds the keys to worshipping the one true God. The volume is replete with pictures of the Lord Jesus Christ and His glorious salvation. It teaches us how imperfect believers can experience and maintain fellowship with an absolutely holy God through proper worship.

By lifting out of Leviticus principles that serve as signposts to guide us, the author leads us on an exciting journey of discovery that begins at Calvary and proceeds into the throne room of heaven itself. Along the way we come to know unfailing wisdom, unspeakable joy, and untarnished fellowship with no less a person than the eternal Son of God.

Dr. John Williamson
Acorn Ridge Baptist Church
Robbins, North Carolina

INTRODUCTION

There is no book in the entire Canon that contains more of the very words of God than the book of Leviticus. God is the direct speaker on almost every page. Leviticus contains a full system of truth. It exhibits sin and the sinner. It teaches of grace and the Savior. It gives clear details of worship and duty.

The key word in this divine book is "holy" and is used 87 times throughout the book. Holiness, by definition, is "the state or condition of being holy, sanctified, consecrated."[i] It denotes being set apart or separated. In its biblical application to God, it depicts the idea of purity and righteousness. Holiness, scripturally, is that mysterious purity and indescribable glory which belongs alone to God and which differentiates Him from all things in His created world. Also, those things which are set apart and dedicated to Him, including men, are invested with holiness (Lev. 11:44). God's command is: *"Ye shall therefore sanctify yourselves..."* that is, we are to set ourselves apart unto God. Is this not what Jesus was instructing us to do when He commanded: *"Seek ye first the kingdom of God and his righteousness"*? (Matt. 6:33). When we make that commitment to put God and His will for our lives first (separation), God informs us that we become holy. Because of man's inclination to renege from such commitments, he must be careful to make reverent use of those means which God has provided for us and are declared in this book.

The theme of the book of Leviticus is the essential elements of worship. Worship is "the honor, reverence, and homage paid to superior beings or powers, whether men, angels or God."[ii] In its application to God, it denotes recognition of His perfection and absolute righteousness. The purpose of the book of Leviticus is to teach man how to get right and then stay right with a holy God. Thus it purposes to teach an elect, holy people how to worship (approach) a holy God and live in fellowship with Him. Louis Goldberg stated it this way: "The theme of the book tells how an elect, holy people should worship a holy God."[iii]

Genesis concludes with a promise: *"And Joseph said unto his brethren, I die; and God will surely visit you, and bring you out of this land unto the land which he sware to Abraham, to Isaac, and to Jacob."* (Gen. 50:24). In Exodus, after the promise concluding Genesis was fulfilled, God said to Israel: "Keep your distance." But now, in Leviticus, God says to them: "You may come into my presence but these are the rules." It is interesting that the word "Leviticus" literally means: "and He called."

Specifically, the purpose of the book of Leviticus is to train and prepare the nation of Israel to fulfill the special historic mission to which God had chosen them: namely, to mediate to the world God's gracious plan of redemption. Is that not also God's gracious plan for the true church in this dispensation of Grace? Thus, the lessons this book teaches are applicable to the church today.

This book teaches three fundamental lessons: the importance of both internal and external separation; the unapproachable holiness of God; and that sacrifice is the basis of true worship. This book makes clear that acceptable worship of God must be based upon a sacrifice that is acceptable to God. Where and how we meet God is important. It is the purpose of this study to assist the reader to learn how God is to be approached and how we may walk in consistent fellowship with Him. Like all truth, we shall discover that the truths of worship are an inverse pyramid with each succeeding truth dependent upon the implementation and sustaining of the previous truths. Isaiah stated this principle so eloquently in Isaiah 28:10 where he said: *"For precept must be upon precept, precept upon precept; line upon line, line upon line; here a little and there a little."* In this study we shall see that God, in the book of Leviticus, lays out for us twelve principles of worship wherein each succeeding truth can only become operational when all preceding truths are in place and operational in the worshipper's life.

This is a journey of faith. Come join me on this awesome journey!

Chapter 1

ABOUT THE BOOK

It is not our intent in this book to study the book of Leviticus verse by verse. As we look at the theme of this book, our plan is to systematically lay out God's instructions to Israel relating to the issue of how to approach Him and walk in His presence. Thus shall we learn how we may truly worship God.

As we begin this study it is important that we have a grasp of the book's outline. Here is a simple outline. Chapters one to seven teach us the truths regarding sacrifice. Chapters eight to ten teach us the truths of consecration. Chapters eleven to fifteen teach us the truths of sanctification. Chapter sixteen teaches us the truth regarding redemption (atonement). Chapters seventeen to twenty-seven instruct us in the ways of holiness. These five elements: sacrifice, consecration, sanctification, atonement and holiness not only give us the outline of Leviticus, but also give us the essentials for true worship as we shall come to see as we study this unique book.

The Essentials for Interpretation

Before we begin this study there are three essentials for us to grasp if we are to fully understand and apply the truths of this book to our own life and practice. First, we must be careful not to mix law and grace, an easy thing to do in the book of Leviticus. Law is a "schoolmaster" which connotes bondage. Paul stated: *"But before faith came, we were kept under the law, shut up unto the faith which should afterwards be revealed. Wherefore the law was our schoolmaster to bring us unto Christ, that we might be justified by faith. But after that faith is come, we are no longer under a schoolmaster."* (Galatians 3:23-25). Grace, however, is "that quality of God's nature which is the source of men's undeserved blessings, in particular those blessings which have to do with their salvation from sin."[iv] The key word is "undeserved" or "not earned". Thus Paul wrote: *"For by grace are ye saved through faith; and that not of yourselves; it is the gift of God: not of works lest any man should boast."* (Ephesians 2:8-9). Thus we must understand that law and grace do not mix. Some years ago, a much respected Bible teacher commented to me: "Ken, there is no grace in Leviticus. It is all law." We shall see that grace does truly abound in this precious book.

Second, in understanding God's Word we must also be aware of the rules for determining a "type". There are three rules. First, a true biblical type must be a true picture of the person or thing it prefigures. There must be an obvious resemblance. Second, a true type must be a divine appointment. It must be divinely designed to bear a likeness to its anti-type. Third, a true type always prefigures something that is yet future.

There are multitudes of illustrations clarifying this important point. Joseph, Jacob's son, and King David were both a type of Christ. Joseph suffered unjustly in order to establish God's plan for Israel's deliverance from bondage. The ancient Rabbis liken Joseph to the line of Messianic prophecies that relate to Messiah's suffering. They taught the coming of two Messiahs: Messiah ben Joseph as the suffering servant and Messiah ben David as the Messiah who would come as king. Both truly picture the Messiah. Joseph depicts the Messiah who would come to suffer and die to be the full, perfect and complete payment for sin. David depicts the Messiah who will one day come to rule and reign not just over Israel, but over the entire world. The Passover lamb, described in Exodus 12 is a type of the Messiah. Notice that in Exodus 12:21 the lamb is described both as "the lamb" and as "the Passover." In 1 Corinthians 5:7 Paul described Jesus as "the Passover." Whereas John, described Jesus as *"the lamb of God that taketh away the sin of the world."* John 1:29.

In Abraham's sacrifice of his son Isaac it took two separate types to complete the type. Isaac was a type of Christ as he was offered up by his father. But it took God's miraculous provision of a ram to complete the type. The ram was both innocent and provided by God Himself. Isaac could not, in his death, fulfill the true type. Thus he was redeemed by the perfect and sinless ram which God, Himself, provided. Messiah was offered up by His Father as the perfect sinless "lamb of God." Isaac's death would have been meaningless as a type of Christ's death as Isaac was not without sin. Thus types are a series of shadows projecting Messiah Jesus. He is the center, the truth of all revelation. (cf. Colossians 2:16-17).

The Author, Date and place of Revelation

There is no doubt that Moses is the human author as it is so stated in Leviticus 1:1. *"The LORD called unto Moses and spake unto him out of the tabernacle of the congregation."* Jesus affirmed it in Matthew 8:4; Luke 24:27, 44; and John 7:19.

Most Bible teachers place the writing of this book in the 15th century B.C. about 1450-1446 B.C. The first Passover occurred on the fourteenth day of the first month of the Exodus. The Tabernacle was erected about one year later (Exodus 40:17). Israel began her journey to Canaan the next month according to Numbers 10:11. Thus Leviticus had to be written just after the erection of the Tabernacle. After the Exodus, God spoke to Moses first out of Mount Sinai (Exodus 19:3). However, Leviticus was delivered to Moses by God speaking out of the newly constructed Tabernacle (Leviticus 1:1).

Where we meet God is important. If we seek Him outside of Messiah Jesus we will only find destruction. But if we meet Him in Messiah Jesus we will find redemption, deliverance from our sin, and fellowship with the only one and true God. In this study we will seek to learn how God is to be approached and how we may walk consistently with Him.

This is a journey of faith.Come join me on this awesome journey.

PART I

THE FOUNDATION FOR WORSHIP

CHAPTER 2

THE FOUNDATION OF WORSHIP # 1

Leviticus 16

Chapter 16 is the supreme chapter of the book of Leviticus, the climax of the whole Mosaic sacrificial system. This chapter is truly the gospel according to Moses. It points up the imperfection and sinfulness even of the most holy acts and services. It shows the necessity even for the cleansing of the place and the utensils used (vv. 18-20a). Then it goes on to show the necessity of atonement first for the priests themselves, the leaders of this holy activity, before atonement could be made for anyone else (vv. 6, 11). This chapter teaches the sinfulness of man, his depravity (his inability to do anything in and of himself to make himself right with God), and his need of a substitute to make atonement on his behalf. Thus atonement is an act of grace received by faith, not of works. It is not what man can do for himself but what God, in His loving grace, is willing to do for man that man may have a personal relationship with Him, the only one and true God.

Worship Defined

Someone once rightly stated: "Worship is man's faith response to God's revealed Grace." It alone emphasizes the primacy of God. Pastor

Edward Drew, in defining worship, stated: "It is the sum total of all your dealings with God. It encompasses your prayer and praise and adoration. It encompasses all you do just for the love of Him."ᵛ Worship, then, is the response of God's creation to the Creator. Worship is not an end in itself as so many believe and have been taught. It is an ongoing responsive relationship between the creature and his Creator.

How to approach the Creator

This chapter gives us the first and necessary step of worship: how to approach the Creator. As we have already stated and seen, God can only be approached on His terms. The Bible clearly teaches us that He is to be approached with fear and reverence. Also, God can only be approached with a clean vessel. This was so eloquently taught by the giving of the ritual to cleanse the priests, the Tabernacle, and the people. There are two very important principles here for us to understand.

The first principle is stated for us in Leviticus 17:11. *"For the life of the flesh is in the blood; and I have given it to you upon the altar to make atonement for your souls: for it is the blood that maketh atonement for your soul."* Thus the first principle is: "Without the shedding of blood there is no atonement for the soul." Moses gave us the reason for this requirement when he later stated: *"For the life of all flesh is the blood thereof."* (Lev. 17:14c). The blood thus represents one's life.

This leads us to the second very important principle we need to understand. I choose to call it "The exchange of life principle." When Adam and Eve sinned in the garden their lives were polluted. Because the sin of Adam is passed down through his seed we are all polluted. Isaiah described man this way: *"But we are all as an unclean thing, and all our righteousnesses are as filthy rags; and we all do fade as a leaf; and our iniquities, like the wind, have taken us away."* (Isaiah 64:6). Note that Isaiah states that our righteousnesses are of no value when it comes to making us acceptable to God. In Isaiah 57:12 Isaiah defined what he meant by "righteousness": *"I will declare thy righteousness, and thy works; for they shall not profit thee."* In Jewish thought a mitzvah involves both righteous living and righteous deeds (works). Here Isaiah shows that neither helps us in the matter of getting right with God. Why? Because God's demand is that we are to be holy because He is holy (cf. Lev.

11:44; 1 Peter 1:16). So when we are living righteously and/or doing righteous deeds (works) we are only doing what is demanded of us. Therefore, our righteousnesses cannot make right what we have done wrongly, whether those wrongs are the way we are living or deeds that we have specifically done. Thus mankind has a major problem in terms of getting right and staying right with his Creator.

This fact necessitates the "exchange of life" principle. God loves us and desires to fellowship with us, not for Himself, but for the blessings that accrue to us in having that fellowship with Him (cf. Psalm 16:11). But He cannot fellowship with us as long as there is unredeemed sin in our life. So God devised a plan whereby both His holiness and His love were satisfied. His plan is called the "Exchange of life." God's plan is to exchange the life of one who is without sin for those who are sin. In the Old Testament economy the exchange took place between an innocent and perfect animal (a goat, lamb or bullock) for the guilty. The animal was slain and its blood sprinkled as an atonement for the sinner. The Hebrew word translated "atonement" is *kawfar* which literally means: "covering" or "to cover over." It has the sense of covering as with pitch. It implies reconciliation. This principle was established almost immediately after Adam and Eve sinned. According to Genesis 3:21, God killed animals to provide Adam and his wife with a covering. Notice that the covering was not necessary until they sinned. So the issue was not just clothing. This was to be understood as a covering for their sin. This truth is reinforced in Genesis chapter 4. Abel's sacrifice was accepted because it involved the shedding of blood according to the "exchange of life" principle established by God with Abel's parents. Because Cain refused to bring the proper sacrifice his offering was not accepted. In the Passover experience, God demonstrated through the physical deliverance of Israel from their bondage in Egypt, man's spiritual deliverance from his bondage in sin. Note that God offered the gift. Israel simply had to believe (cf. Exodus 12:13, 23, 27, 50). It is a gift of Grace received by faith. There is nothing that man can do to make himself right with God. God does it all and we must receive it by faith.

The atonement sacrifices of the Mosaic system were intended by God to both illustrate and point to the one ultimate sacrifice that He would offer in the sending of His only Son to suffer and die on Calvary, not for Himself, but for us. In Isaiah 53 this principle is stated over and over (six times). We perhaps know it better as the vicarious atonement. Daniel prophesied it in Daniel 9:24. Their sins were not cleansed by the animal sacrifice but by their faith acceptance of the Divine sacrifice God would one day provide. They were only covered until the ultimate sacrifice was offered and divinely received. On the Day of Atonement everyone was to seek forgiveness (atonement) for all sin, intentional and unintentional.

Exposition of Chapter 16

In verses one and two God gave Moses instructions for Aaron, his brother. Aaron was not allowed to enter into the holy place whenever he wanted. This was illustrated when Aaron's two sons entered into the Holy Place to offer incense before the Lord which the Lord had not commanded them to do and the Lord destroyed them. To enter uninvited into the Holy Place is to beckon God's judgment as with Aaron's two sons, Nadab and Abihu. Herein the holiness of God was impressed upon Aaron.

Verses three to five list for us the things that were necessary for this ceremony. Four things are listed for Aaron, the High Priest, who was the central figure in this ceremony and three things for the congregation. Aaron was to present a young bullock as a sin offering and a ram for a burnt offering. He was further required to wear sacred garments made of plain linen, which typifies righteousness, as a servant. He was to be seen simply as the head for the people. Before he could put on the sacred garments he was required to bathe, an act of symbolic purification reminding the High Priest of his need for atonement. The congregation was to bring two he-goats as a sin offering and one ram as a burnt offering.

Verses seven to ten describe for us what was to be done with the two he-goats. The two goats were to be placed at the door of the Tabernacle. Lots were to be cast to determine which goat would be slain. The chosen goat was then prepared as a sin offering. This was the means of reconciliation with God. Here we see the "Exchange of Life" principle enacted. The second goat was driven out into the desert. It is called *Azazel* which means scapegoat. This signified dismissal or removal of the sins of the people both from them and from the presence of the Holy God. Together, these two features of the sin offering depicted the full meaning of atonement. These actions spoke of both the necessity of an innocent victim dying for the guilty and the resulting sin being removed to never again be held against the guilty party.

Verses eleven to twenty-nine describe the ceremony in more detail. Verses eleven to fourteen describe the ceremony for Aaron and his house. First, the bullock was killed pointing out the necessity of death to make atonement. Then burning coals and sweet incense were placed behind the veil symbolizing prayer. A cloud of incense was made in the Holy of Holies so that the Mercy Seat was hidden and Aaron was protected from the danger of death. The blood was then sprinkled representing forgiveness and the gift of new life which only God is able to provide. Notice how the blood was sprinkled: once on the front of the Mercy Seat indicating that it is sprinkled Godward; and seven times in front of the Mercy Seat acknowledging the need of atonement for the priest's ministry before God. This represents the cleansing of the holiest place defiled by the sins of Aaron, the High Priest. Thus we see that in humility and prayer the High Priest was to seek acceptance by God. It is an interesting fact here that Aaron was instructed to approach God first with prayer (incense) and then with the blood. In verse fourteen we see the presentation of the blood of the bullock which represents by identification a new life for the High Priest. Again, we see the "Exchange of Life" principle in action. Thus we note that his own sin had to be atoned for before the High Priest could offer the atonement sacrifice for the congregation. Should not those of us who serve to lead others in worship take note of this important issue?

Verses fifteen to nineteen indicate that the first goat offered by the congregation provided the atonement for Israel, again demonstrating the "Exchange of Life" principle. The High Priest was to follow the same order of events for the congregation as he was required to do for himself. He did it also for the Tabernacle showing that sin pollutes everything it touches even the altar of burnt sacrifice (vv 18- 19). This was the truth that Paul was demonstrating when he wrote: "*Moreover he sprinkled with blood both the tabernacle and the vessels of the ministry. And almost all things are by the law purged with blood; and without the shedding of blood is no remission.*" (Hebrews 9:21-22). Paul went on to show that, because these ancient sacrifices were temporary, it was necessary for Christ to come to offer once and forever a complete and eternal sacrifice for sin. We are also called to note the loneliness of the work of the High Priest as stated in verse seventeen. It is interesting that the atonement of an entire nation depended upon one man indicating that the atonement for an entire world also depended upon one man.

Verses twenty to twenty-two deal with the second goat. Following the atonement their attention was turned to the live goat which now deals with man's conscience. Aaron laid his hands upon the goat and confessed all of the sins of Israel thus symbolically transferring all of the guilt of Israel to the goat. We are told that a fit man, one appointed for the purpose, led the goat out into the wilderness. He later returned and attested that he left the goat in the wilderness. Jewish tradition tells us that the goat was often taken out into the wilderness and driven over a precipice so that it could not possibly return indicating that, through the atonement sacrifice, our sins are forever removed from us to never again be held against us. In verses twenty-three and twenty-four this act was the testimony of the completeness of the transaction. Aaron was to take off his linen garb; bathe and put on his usual clothing. Then he offered a burnt offering both for himself and for the people. This indicates the dedication of his whole heart and innermost desires unto God. Access into God's presence is now opened!

Verses twenty-five to twenty-eight give three additional directions. The fat of the sin offering was burned. The one who escorted the scapegoat must now wash himself and his clothes, at which time he was then allowed back into the camp. This further signifies the separation of the sins upon the scapegoat. The residue of the animal sacrifices was then burned outside the camp. Now all was done, leaving Israel with the assurance of their sins forgiven and the way opened into the presence of the Holy God.

In verses twenty-nine to thirty-four it is stated that Atonement by the blood is an everlasting statute. Here God clearly means "forever." This day is enjoined to be a Sabbath Day. They were to do no servile work indicating an outward observance. They were further enjoined to "afflict their soul" indicating heart or inward observance. After the destruction of the Temple this came to mean a day of fasting, prayer, and searching of the soul as the means of atonement. Though this may demonstrate a searching for God, according to Moses' instruction it is not enough to effect atonement for sin as this was to be an observance after sin had been atoned for through the blood sacrifice. Without the blood sacrifice fasting, prayer and the searching of the soul is meaningless in terms of atoning for one's sins.

The New Life

This new life provided for us by God Himself through the sacrifice of His Lamb, Jesus, can only be received through an act of faith (believing). Faith must have an object, that is, something in which we exercise our faith. John stated it in this manner: *"For whatsoever is born of God overcometh the world: and this is the victory that overcometh the world, even our faith. Who is he that overcometh the world but he that believeth that Jesus is the Son of God."* (I John 5:4-5). The object of saving faith is Jesus, the Son of God. Apart from accepting His deity one cannot be saved. As deity Jesus gave His perfect life as the just payment for our sin. Only God can be sinless. Only the sacrifice of a sinless man could make a perfect sacrifice.

Thus one cannot be saved by simply offering a ritual prayer. First, there must be a change of heart constituting a change of focus. It is necessary for one to agree with God about one's condition of sin. Only the Holy Spirit can convict of sin. He does it through the reading or hearing of God's precious word. Then, in order to be saved, by the working of the Holy Spirit one must recognize and receive the redeeming work of God's Son accomplished at Calvary as the only full and complete payment for sin. This must be the focus of our faith (trust or belief). Perhaps a simple prayer from the heart would go something like this: "Oh God, I am helpless and undone. Oh God, for Jesus sake, save me." This prayer is the cry of a needy heart that recognizes that only God, through Christ and what He accomplished on the Cross, can do what he so desperately needs to have done for him.

A man, who had lived a drunken life, after he was saved, shared this testimony: "When God saved me He changed my d'ruthers." When we are truly saved our focus is changed. Paul described the transformation brought about by a new focus like this: *"Therefore if any man be in*

Christ, he is a new creature: old things are passed away; behold all things are become new." (II Corinthians 5:17). Through this change of direction caused by our honest trusting in Christ and His sacrifice on Calvary we are separated from sin to fellowship with God (cf. Hebrews 10:10). As a result of our exercised faith in Christ there is a clear change of desire and direction for our life (cf. Hebrews 11:13-16; 24-26). One example is Abraham who, in faith, forsook his old life which was centered in idol worship to embrace a new life in serving God (cf. Hebrews 11:8-10). To truly receive Christ as Saviour we must turn from our unbelief and trust Jesus as the only way to be saved in order to receive the new life in Christ. Remember, true repentance involves both a turning from and a turning to. (cf. Acts 3:19; II Peter 3:9; Acts 20:21; Matthew 9:13; Luke 13:3-5).

This opens the door for us to truly worship. *"Having therefore, brethren, boldness to enter into the holiest by the blood of Jesus, by a new and living way, which he hath consecrated for us, through the veil, that is to say, his flesh; and having a high priest over the house of God; let us draw near with a true heart in full assurance of faith, having our hearts sprinkled from an evil conscience, and our bodies washed with pure water."* (Hebrews 10:19-22). With this begins our awesome journey. Have you truly experienced a change of heart that brought to you a change of direction?

If not, why not right now agree with God about your sin condition? The Holy Spirit will enable you if you are willing. Then, by faith, gladly receive Christ as the sacrifice for your sin and step into His presence and begin this awesome journey of faith.

Lessons to be learned

The first lesson here to be learned is that God allows mankind to approach Him only on His terms. All roads do not lead to Rome. This chapter of God's word clearly teaches that there is only one way: God's way. Thus Atonement (reconciliation) can be made for sin only through the shedding of the blood of an innocent victim. This process is seen as the "exchange of life" principle. We see that our reconciliation is dependent upon one person completing the process perfectly on our behalf (in Leviticus it was the High Priest); for us, it is Jesus. Speaking of the priestly sacrifices Paul stated: *"which was a figure for the time present, in which were offered both gifts and sacrifices, that could not make him that did the service perfect, as pertaining to the conscience; which stood only in meats and drinks, and divers washings, and carnal ordinances, imposed on them until the time of reformation. But Christ being come an High Priest of good things to come, by a greater and more perfect tabernacle, not made with hands, that is to say, not of this building; neither by the blood of goats and calves, but by his own blood he entered in once into the holy place, having obtained eternal redemption for us."* (Hebrews 9:9-12). He goes on to say in verse fourteen: *"How much more shall the blood of Christ, who through the eternal Spirit offered himself without spot to God, purge your conscience from dead works to serve the living God?"*

The second lesson we must grasp is that the word "atonement" as used in the Old Testament (particularly in Leviticus) does not have precisely the same meaning as the word "reconciliation" found in the New Testament. It does mean "the bringing together of two who have been enemies into a relationship of peace and friendship."[vi] But reconciliation is "a change of relationship between God and man based on the changed status of man through the redemptive work of Christ."[vii] The Hebrew word translated "atonement" is *kaphar* which literally means "to cover". We must be reminded that no one is saved through the works of the law. God's purpose in commanding the sacrificial system was to give Israel something concrete that pointed them to the one sacrifice that God Himself would one day make. They were to understand that the sacrifices were not an end in themselves, but that they were to trust in the sacrifice that God promised would not just cover but remove their sin from them. Thus Old Testament saints were saved by looking forward to Calvary while, since the sacrifice was made, we are privileged to look back to it and be saved. The "covering" was necessary at that time in order for God to have a relationship with man and man with Him until He presented His lamb as the full and complete payment for all sin.

One final lesson is also clearly taught here. The congregation cannot truly worship and be blessed if the priest (the leader) is not himself right with God. That is certainly depicted by the necessity for Aaron to be fully cleansed before he could effectively serve the people. How important it is, then, for the pastor and other worship leaders to be absolutely sure they are saved and sanctified in His presence before they seek to lead the people in this awesome experience of public worship.

We have learned that sin pollutes everything it touches. But sin, divinely forgiven, is sin never again to be remembered against us. Thus salvation not only involves forgiveness of sin but a total commitment to the one who cleanses us. We must believe that what He did for us is fully effected.

Thus the first principle of worship is the necessity of redemption. Apart from being cleansed of our sin nature inherited from Adam and our sinful deeds, we cannot worship God. It is not that the old sin nature is eradicated at the point of salvation because it is not. We are given the indwelling Holy Spirit so that we can overcome the sin nature. Paul stated: *"Likewise reckon ye also yourselves to be dead indeed unto sin, but alive unto God through Jesus Christ our Lord."* (Romans 6:11).

Apart from being redeemed one cannot approach a holy God. Have you been redeemed? Do you know the joy of having been made whole and set free? If so, you have made the first step on this awesome journey of faith called worship.

CHAPTER 3

THE FOUNDATION FOR WORSHIP # 2

Leviticus 4:1-5:13; 6:24-30

Let us remember that worship, simply, is "man's faith response to God's revealed grace." One biblical illustration of what worship is may be found in Psalm 23:6 where David stated: *"Surely goodness and mercy shall follow me all the days of my life: and I will dwell in the house of the Lord forever."* David, in Psalm 16:11 stated the divine purpose in creating man in the first place: *"Thou wilt show me the path of life: in thy presence is fullness of joy; at thy right hand are pleasures for evermore."* God's intent for creating man was that He might fellowship with man and man with Him. That is exactly what the life of faith (worship) is all about. In Psalm 23 David was not talking about taking up residence in the Tabernacle (God's house). He was talking about living in the presence of the Almighty God. It is interesting in Psalm 16:11 that David indicates there are at least two levels of relationship man may have with his Creator. We will learn more about that as we progress through this study. But now let us turn our attention to the second foundational principle of worship.

As we have learned in the previous chapter, in order to worship the only one true God, we must first be redeemed from the just eternal penalty of our sin. We saw that this is only accomplished through an act of grace by God Himself on our behalf, the "exchange of life" principle, which we can receive only by faith. This act of God's grace received by faith establishes for us the capacity for living in His presence as He imparts to us His divine nature. In fact, the moment we believe, we are both brought into His presence and given His divine nature. The issue now before us is how we maintain that relationship in good standing.

The issue that confronts us at this point is the continuing issue of sin. The unfortunate truth is that we all still sin, even after we have been saved. Though our eternal destiny with God through Christ is never in jeopardy after we are saved our fellowship is broken by the smallest of sins. As true worship is living in His presence (not just an act on Sundays) a right relationship must be maintained. As God cannot tolerate sin, even the minutest perceived sin, our ongoing sin problem must be confronted. That is what we will now consider as God shows us what is needful through the Mosaic sin sacrifice system which was intended to deal with both accidental sins and sins of ignorance.

The Sin Offerings

First, Leviticus chapter four deals with accidental sins: *"If a soul shall sin through ignorance against any of the commandments of the Lord concerning things which aught not to be done, and shall do against any of them:"* (v. 2). These are acts committed but not understood at the time to be sin. So the offering he is about to describe is an offering of expiation. Expiation is an act whereby sin is canceled and fellowship is restored. This is not an atonement sacrifice. Atonement establishes the relationship. Expiation restores the relationship when it is broken.

Here is a simple outline of chapter four. Verses 1-2: Introduction; verses 3-12: The Sin Offering for the High Priest; verses 13-21: The Sin Offering for the congregation; verses 22-26: The Sin Offering for a Prince or Ruler; verses 27-35: The Sin Offering for a common person.

Notice two things: It does not matter if you are the High Priest, a prince or ruler, or just a common person. There is no respecter of persons with God. Everyone sins. Everyone is held accountable. The sins here dealt with are not sins of omission, but acts committed by a person when, at the time, he did not recognize the deeds as sin. It is also noteworthy that again God begins with the necessity of the high priest to be in good standing with Him before the high priest can minister to the people. What an awesome responsibility a pastor has! In order for him to function in God's will in relation to his congregation he must consistently stay sanctified.

The Sin Offering Explained

The sin offering required for the high priest was no less than that for the whole congregation (cf. v. 14). He was to bring a young bullock without blemish (cf. v.3). Notice the order of events. First, the priest brought the bullock to the door of the tabernacle. So the bullock is presented outside the Tabernacle. He then laid his hands upon the bullock's head symbolizing the transfer of the sin or sins to the bullock which was then killed. The blood was caught in a basin, carried into the Tabernacle where it was *sprinkled* seven times before the veil. Some of the blood was then put upon the horns of the altar with the rest poured out at the bottom of the altar of burnt offering. The fat, kidneys, and liver (caul) were then taken and burned upon the altar of burnt offering as was to be done in the Peace Offering. What was left of the bullock was then taken outside and burned.

The essence for the removal of all sin, be it at the point of redemption or after the fact, was the shed blood of an innocent animal (the "exchange of life" principle). The sprinkling of the blood seven times denotes a perfect or complete action. This is precisely what John taught in his first epistle when he wrote: *"If we confess our sins, he is faithful and just to forgive us and to cleanse us from all unrighteousness."* (I John 1:9). In the first two verses of chapter two John depicts for us a courtroom scene with God as the judge, Satan as the prosecuting attorney and Christ as the believer's defense attorney. Satan rightly accuses us. Christ does not seek to make excuses for us. He simply states: "Father, I have shed my blood for this sin." The purpose of the sin sacrifice being likened to the peace offering indicates assurance that the issue is resolved. The significance of the remaining blood being poured out at the altar of burnt offering confirms that God has accepted us back into His sweet fellowship based upon the blood. The burning of the remains signifies the complete destruction that sin brings indicating that the issue is now totally resolved.

The sin offering for the congregation (4:13-21) follows the same procedure except it is the elders of the people who were required to lay hands on the bullock before it was killed. This was to signify the transfer of the sins of the people to the bullock. For the priest and the congregation the blood was sprinkled on the altar of incense. Note again the "exchange of life" principle even for unintentional sins.

There were some things that were to be different for a prince or ruler (4:22-26). The animal required was a male kid from the goats. It is important to note that the offerer was required to kill it making him responsible for the death of the substitute. This was a humiliating experience, signifying the importance of a humble spirit in seeking forgiveness. Here the blood is sprinkled on the altar of burnt offering. The rest of the process was the same as for the priest.

The sin offering for a common person required a female kid from the goats (4:27-35). This constituted a great sacrifice because of the loss of any future offspring. This indicates how costly sin is. The process is the same as for the prince or ruler. Again, it is important to note that in each case the requirements strike at the very heart of what is dear to the offerer.

The altar of Incense in the Holy Place was peculiarly the scene of the priest's intercession and of the people's prayers as a congregation. The sins in holy things pointed inward toward the Holy Place, whereas a ruler's sins or those of the common people pointed toward the camp.

Thus the blood of their offering was sprinkled on the horns of the altar where it would be publicly observed.

Sins of Negligence

Again, a blood sacrifice depicting a vicarious payment through the shedding of innocent blood was required (the "exchange of life" principle). The order of the process is laid out for us. In this ritual it was necessary to confess the specific sin (cf. verse 5). He then would present his trespass offering and the animal would be killed with the blood sprinkled on the side of the altar with the rest poured out at the base of the altar.

In verses 11 to 13 we are informed of God's grace to those who were too poor to bring a blood sacrifice. They were allowed to bring a grain offering. This was clearly a substitute for the better offering, signifying that God's grace is available to all regardless of their status. Through this ritual the worshipper was to look forward to the Day of Atonement to complete that for which this offering was a substitute. An "ephah" represented one day's needs. Thus the worshipper was required to fast one day in order to make this sacrifice. No frankincense was allowed with this offering. The purpose of this was to present both the worshipper and his offering as altogether defiled. The memorial part of the offering was consumed by fire. The rest of the offering the priest was allowed to keep, because the sin was cleansed out of the worshipper.

In every case the offender presented the sacrifice, confessed his sins and placed his hands on the head of the victim. This signified that the worshipper identified himself with the sacrifice and that his guilt was thus transferred to the offering. Again, we see the absolute necessity of the "exchange of life" principle when it comes to the matter of dealing with any sin.

Lessons to be Learned

Expiation is necessary even for one sin and is to be applied the moment the sin becomes known. The reason is simple as stated by James: *"For whosoever shall keep the whole law, and yet offend in one point, he is guilty of all."* (James 2:10). We also need to understand that different grades of offerings do not imply different standards of morality. No one is so obscure that his sin is overlooked or so prominent that his fault is condoned. For each worshipper it was to be a costly sacrifice.

Again, we see the absolute importance of the "exchange of life" principle at work in relation to our daily walk. All sin must be exchanged for His life (Yeshua, Jesus), if we are to maintain a relationship of communion (worship) with God. It is also to be noted that, in order to keep a short account with God, we are required to confess our specific sin(s). It is not enough to just say: "Lord I have sinned." Confession requires admitting the specific sin so that we may be truly repentant.

We further note that the animal whose blood was used to expiate sin could not be eaten. It was totally polluted by the transfer of sin. Only the meat of the offerings for sin presented by rulers or members of the congregation could be eaten by the priest. All bodies of other sin offerings were burnt outside the camp. The difference is the animal presented. It is the blood of bulls that is taken into the Tabernacle. The blood of other animals was not taken into the Tabernacle. Thus, as that which was offered was holy, so, as the priests ate that portion set aside for them by an act of God's grace, they, too, were set apart as holy. It could only be eaten by the priests in the courtyard of the Tabernacle.

The sin offering covered accidental and ignorant sins. But for one who sinned willfully in clear open rebellion against God there was no offering. Note what the author of Hebrews wrote: *"For if we sin willfully after that we have received the knowledge of the truth, there remaineth no more sacrifice for sins, but a certain fearful looking for of judgment and fiery indignation, which shall devour the adversaries."* (Hebrews 10:26-27). John helps us to understand this concept when he wrote: *"We know that whosoever is born of God sinneth not; but he that is begotten of God keepeth himself, and that wicked one toucheth him not."* (I John 5:18). What John has stated here is that one who has truly been born again will not sin habitually. This is in agreement with what Paul wrote to the Corinthians in his second epistle: *"Therefore if any man be in Christ, he is a new creature: old things are passed away; behold, all things are become new."* (II Cor. 5:17).

So, we see the absolute necessity for both atonement (redemption) and expiation (cleansing). This is the message of Jesus to His disciples as recorded in John 13. Jesus started to wash the feet of His disciples. Peter objected. Jesus responded to him that if He were not allowed to wash his feet Peter would have no part in Him. Then Peter said: *"Lord, not my feet only, but also my hands and my head."* (John 13:9). To this Jesus replied: *"He that is washed needeth not save to wash his feet, but is clean every whit: and ye are clean, but not all."* (v. 10). If you have had the bath (been saved) you only need an occasional washing to have your inadvertent sins dealt with.

In one complete sacrifice Jesus made atonement for all sin, past, present, and future. Our responsibility is to receive it by faith, then maintain the resulting fellowship by keeping a short account with God (cf. Hebrews 9:11-12; I John 1:9-2:2). Thus we learn the second principle of worship. Only he who keeps sin cleansed from his life can truly worship (have fellowship with) God. This can only occur after we have truly been born again. You cannot enjoy the second principle without first having experienced the first. You see, worship is an awesome walk of faith.

We have now learned the first two principles necessary for establishing and basically maintaining a personal relationship with our Creator. There are ten more principles we need to learn and apply if we are to grow in our relationship with Him. So let us move forward with this awesome walk of faith!

PART II

THE ATTITUDE OF WORSHIP

CHAPTER 4

DEDICATION OF LIFE

Leviticus Chapter 1; 6:8-13

If one is to truly worship God he must first be born anew through the precious blood of the Lord Jesus, Israel's Messiah. This is the point at which worship is established. But if worship is living in His presence, sin must be dealt with thus making the keeping of a short account with God an absolute necessity. These two principles are foundational to establishing and maintaining a worship relationship with the Creator God.

David, in Psalm 16:11, teaches us that there are two levels of fellowship we may have with God. *"In thy presence is fullness of joy; at thy right hand are pleasures for evermore."* In ancient times, to be at the king's right hand denoted an intimate relationship. David tells us that there is "fullness of joy" in just being in our Lord's presence. When we develop an intimate relationship with Him we will experience unending pleasures.

If we are already living the first two principles we should be experiencing joy. All of the principles that follow will enable our worship relationship with God to be both strengthened and deepened so that we may enjoy the blessings of an intimate relationship with Him. So, let us move on in this awesome journey of faith.

The Whole Burnt Offering

The next principle is clearly illustrated in the teachings related to the whole burnt offering. It is important to note that this is a voluntary offering. God said to Moses: *"If any man of you bring an offering unto the LORD"* (v. 2). The Hebrew word translated "if" could also be properly translated "when" indicating that this offering about to be described is voluntary. The Hebrew word *qorban,* which means "offering" or "gift", also points up the voluntary nature of the burnt offering. Verse 3 clearly states it: *"He shall offer it of his own voluntary will."* The fact that nothing of this sacrifice was left undestroyed indicates that the essential feature of this offering is dedication.

The animal had to be from the possessions of the worshipper, that is, from that which belonged to him. The gift was to be offered on the basis of one's economic stature, that is, on the basis of what he possessed. It was to be the most expensive gift he could offer (It was to be a perfect male). The acceptable animals were a bullock, a sheep, a goat, a turtledove or young pigeon.

Conditions of Acceptance

Verse four states: *"And he shall put his hand upon the head of the burnt offering; and it shall be accepted for him to make atonement for him."* Here we again see the "exchange of life" principle: the animal's life for the life of the worshipper. The laying of the worshipper's hands on the animal dedicated it to death. It signified transference of the obligation to suffer for sin from the worshipper to the innocent victim. The verb "to lay" in Hebrew is *samak* which literally means "to sustain or support." It is a picture of the worshipper resting (relying) upon the victim to obtain from God that for which it was presented: acceptance by God. It also pictures an acceptance of God's judgment of the worshipper's sinfulness. Thus it implies the worshipper's thankful acceptance of God's offer of grace. This, for the worshipper, is again an act of faith. It demonstrates that the worshipper is depending on the sacrifice to provide him acceptance by a holy God. Here is a picture of total commitment or dedication. Note the words of Jesus, on this point: *"Come unto me, all ye that labor and are heavy laden, and I will give you rest. Take my yoke upon you, and learn of me; for I am meek and lowly in heart; and ye shall find rest unto your souls."* (Matt 11:28-29). In these words Jesus encouraged His followers to make a full commitment of life to Him.

The Significance of this Sacrifice

The complete burning of the sacrifice demonstrates the total commitment of the worshipper. To God the worshipper is saying: "My life is not my own. It is yours, God, to do with as you will." It is interesting that the worshipper had to willingly bring his offering in person (vv. 2 -3). Others can lead us. But no one can worship for us. It is a personal act that, in many ways, will be visible to all.

Worship, then, is dependent upon our grateful acceptance of God's offer of grace. God does not force His grace on anyone. We are asked to willingly and gratefully receive it. Acceptance of God's grace results in a voluntary response. The more one experiences God's grace, the greater will be his love for Him and his desire to live pleasing unto Him.

Thus our proper response to God's bestowal of grace is a voluntary total dedication of our life to Him (cf. John 14:15, 21, 23). However, we must understand that the consecration that God asks of us is not merely a single, once-forever act. It must be continuously renewed every morning and every evening based upon the fact that we have willingly presented *"our bodies a living sacrifice, holy and acceptable unto God"* (Rom. 12:1). He has bought us with a price: the life of His only son. After we have been truly saved, our walk with Him really begins when we make this commitment and offer our whole self, body and soul, to Him.

The fire on the brazen altar was never to go out (cf. Lev. 6:12-13). A burnt offering was to be presented every morning and every evening (cf. Lev. 6:9). This was to be a continual burnt offering. Thus we are to keep the fire of our total commitment burning by daily and continuously placing our life on His altar in total dedication.

The third principle of Worship

To truly worship, then, we must recognize that our life is not our own. It belongs to God. We need to further understand that we are called to continuously yield ourselves with total abandonment to the known will of God. Was this not Paul's admonition to us when he wrote to the Church of Rome: *"I beseech you therefore, brethren, by the mercies of God, that ye present your bodies a living sacrifice, holy, acceptable unto God, which is your reasonable service. And be not conformed to this world: but be ye transformed by the renewing of your mind, that ye may prove that good, and acceptable, and perfect, will of God."* (Rom. 12:1-2)? See also Romans 6:11-14. This is a voluntary act that will move us into a more intimate relationship with our Creator and bring us the added blessings He promised us through David.

Let us review: Only one who has been redeemed by the precious blood of Israel's Messiah, the Lord Jesus, can worship. Only one, having been redeemed, can maintain worship by keeping a short account with God thus keeping his sins (specific) confessed (cf. I John 1:9). The worship experience can only grow and become more pure as we consistently keep our life fully dedicated unto Him. This cannot happen until the first two principles are operational in our life. Yes, worship truly is an awesome journey of faith. Are you ready to move on to the next step in our journey?

CHAPTER 5

DEDICATION OF LABOR

Leviticus chapter 2 and 6:14-18

We have, thus far, learned the means of getting right with God and also how to stay right with Him. In the last chapter we began moving into the deeper, more blest life which necessitates the complete dedication of our life to Him (cf. Romans 12: 1-2). This, then, becomes foundational to all of the other principles we shall learn as we move forward on this awesome journey of faith.

If we have totally dedicated our life to God, this will lead us to also dedicate all of our labor to Him. This does not mean that everyone is to become a pastor or a vocational missionary. But it does mean that all we do and the results of what we do are to be dedicated to God that He might be glorified through our daily living. This principle of worship is taught us through the meat offering.

The Meat Offering

The meat offering is presented to us essentially in Leviticus chapter 2. As was the burnt offering, the meat offering is voluntary. It was to be of fine flour. Upon this fine flour was poured oil and sprinkled with frankincense. The Hebrew word that has been translated "meat offering" is the word *minchah* which simply means "offering or "present". This offering was generally made in connection with an animal sacrifice (cf. Lev. 5:13). The essential feature was a gift presented to God.

The Significance

This offering represented the offerer's person and possessions. It could not be offered until all sin had been atoned for. They were to use the best of their grain. It was to be crushed and finely sifted to remove all impurities. This fine flour represents the fruit of one's labors.

Oil was poured over the flour signifying a setting apart. This was Jacob's purpose when he took the stone he had used for a pillow at Bethel creating a pillar which he anointed with oil to commemorate his vision (Genesis 28:18-22). When a priest or the King was anointed with oil it was intended to symbolize that they were set apart unto God. Thus this act signified the offering to be set apart (sanctified) unto God further depicting that a man's labor and the fruit of that labor was to be set apart unto God.

Only one filled with God's Spirit could possibly do this. It is impossible for a man who is full of himself to be a vessel capable of being filled with the Holy Spirit. Thus it follows that one must be emptied of himself in order to be filled with the Spirit. That is the essence of the previous principle of worship. One must be emptied of himself, set apart unto God (sanctified), before he can be empowered to live for Him. In the case of this offering, the oil signified that it was set apart unto God. And, this in turn, indicated that the one making the offering had already made that dedication of his life to God and was thus empowered by God's Spirit enabling him to dedicate his labor and the fruits thereof unto God.

The frankincense exemplifies the acceptableness of the offering. viii The sweet aroma was thought to be pleasing unto God. It further symbolizes prayer and praise. Thus our life, when fully dedicated unto Him, becomes a sweet aroma exuding prayer and praise to the Almighty God.

The Process

The freewill offering was brought to the priests. One handful was taken by the priest and placed on the altar. Oil was poured upon it with frankincense and then it was burned. The remnant of the offering was given by God's direction to the priests for their use. From this we learn that Israel was never to assume that they supported the priests. They, in obedience, willingly gave to God. God, in turn, gave to the priests their portion. When you give your tithes and offerings to whom are you giving them? Are you giving them to the church, the missionary or mission agency? Or are you giving them to God through those channels?

The Varieties

According to verses four to six they could bring oven- baked cakes. Verse seven also suggests that the cakes could be fried. There were two restrictions and one requirement that should be noted. Verse eleven tells us that it could have no leaven in it. Leaven was a symbol of corruption which is symbolic of sin. It also represented carnality and malice (I Cor. 5:8).

The second prohibition was of honey (vs. 11). Honey was also connected to the corruption process. Andrew Bonar stated: Honey "is forbidden both because it turns to sourness, and leads to fermentation, and perhaps also because it is a luxury; and the Lord desires nothing of earthly sweetness. His offerings must have neither corruption nor carnal sweetness."[ix]

There was to be no leaven and no honey. But they were to use salt (vs. 13). Salt was a preservative and cleansing agent. God emphasizes that salt must be used. It was required. Salt purified, positively flavored, cleansed, and was used for healing. It stopped corruption and fermentation. That was the use Jesus gave to it when He said that true believers are "the salt of the earth" (Matt. 5:13). Jesus understood the Mosaic system. Of salt He stated: *"For everyone shall be salted with fire and every sacrifice shall be salted with salt. Salt is good: but if the salt have lost its saltness, wherewith will ye season it? Have salt in yourselves and have peace one with another."* (Mark 9:49-50). The believer's salt is God's word that purifies us as we read it, receive it, and apply it to our daily lives. This offering, representing our labor and the fruits thereof, must be, in its very essence, pure.

Special Regulations for First fruits

If this offering was related to the celebration of First Fruits there were certain other rules that applied according to verses twelve to sixteen. This offering was not to be burnt on the altar for a sweet savor. The corn offered must be green ears dried by the fire (vs. 14). This was a sign of the changeless, incorruptible covenant between God and His people. They were to be beaten out of full ears. Again, oil was poured upon the offering indicting that it was set apart unto God with frankincense sprinkled upon it symbolizing God's acceptance of the offering.

Special Regulations for the Priests

In chapter six, verses fourteen through twenty-three we find special regulations for the priests. First, a memorial portion was burnt signifying the sanctification of the offerer. The rest was the priest's portion to be eaten in the Court of Tabernacles with unleavened bread. As a part of the ritual relating to the anointing of the High Priest, the offering was to be totally consumed.

Lessons to be Learned

Herein Israel was taught that their labor was to be dedicated unto God. They were further taught that their free-will giving was a gift unto God, not to the priests or the Tabernacle. If we have truly dedicated our lives fully to serve and honor God, then our labor and the fruit of it must also be dedicated unto Him. When we give to support God's work we are to view that gift as given to Him, not to a person or agency.

We are also to view all of the fruit of our labor as belonging to Him. Perhaps this would cause us to pray more before making decisions as to how we use the blessings He has bestowed upon us. It should move us to ask the question: "Is it something I really need?" "Will this expenditure honor Him?" Why should we not recognize that all we have belongs to Him and seek His face in how we use it? After all, does

He not have our best interest at heart? Yes, all that we do needs to be seen as done unto God for His glory.

The Fourth Principle of Worship

Thus the fourth principle of worship is the recognition that all our labor and the fruit thereof belongs to Him. Remember, worship, in its fullest sense, is walking (living) in His presence (cf. Psalm 16:11). What a privilege to be free to take everything, every decision, every concern to Him who has only our best interest at heart. Surely this will move us closer to Him and enable us to worship Him more deeply.

Have you made that commitment? Then let us move another step forward in this awesome journey of faith.

CHAPTER 6

THANKSGIVING AND PRAISE

Leviticus 3; 7:11-21, 28-34; 19:5-8

Thus far we have learned that without being saved one cannot worship. This is the message of the Day of Atonement. Salvation (the new birth) establishes our relationship with God. But that is not enough as worship is an ongoing relationship with God. The moment we are truly saved we become His child (cf. John 10:27-29; Hebrews 10:14). But, as God hates sin, fellowship with Him is broken the moment that we sin. So, in order to maintain a relationship with God we must keep our sins confessed. That is the message of the sin offering. It is important and necessary to keep our life cleansed of sin if we are to maintain a worship relationship with God. These, we learned, are the two foundational principles of worship. As we grow in this awesome worship relationship it is necessary that we understand the importance of a life dedicated (committed) to Him. After all, He bought and paid for us. Why should we not give Him our life to serve and honor Him? This is the message of the Burnt Offering. Not only do we need to dedicate our life to Him in service, but we also need to dedicate the fruit of our labor to Him. This is the message of the Meat Offering. When we begin to put these four principles into operation in our life it leads us to a real desire to offer God our thanksgiving and praise. This is the essence of the Peace Offering.

The Peace Offering

The Peace Offering, like the meat offering, is voluntary. Thanksgiving and praise are responses to God's graciousness and goodness. Andrew Bonar, in his commentary on Leviticus, succinctly states the connection between the previous offerings and the peace offering: "The connection is simply this: a justified soul, devoted to the Lord in all things, spontaneously engages in acts of praise and exercises of fellowship, for the soul has been accepted, and is at peace with God."ˣ

This offering required an animal that was without spot or blemish that was taken from the cattle, sheep or goats. Thus, for this offering, they were to give of their best. After all, this was to be an expression of gratitude (thanksgiving) and praise.

In the ritual for this offering, the one making the offering laid his hands upon the offering before it was killed indicating his personal identification with it. Then he had to personally kill it. Regardless of which animal was offered the richest portions were to be offered. The significance here is that the most valuable part of the animal belonged to God. This was called the memorial portion.

The memorial portion included four parts of the animal. The fat was reserved unto God because of its peculiar sanctity. It could not be eaten (cf. Lev. 3:16-17). The kidneys and the caul (the digestive organs) were also dedicated unto the Lord. If the offering was a lamb from the flock the rump was to be dedicated as the memorial portion. The memorial portion was to be burned upon the altar for the daily sacrifice (verse 5). The peace offering was placed on top of the burnt offering as a reminder that one's daily praise and thanksgiving was to be founded afresh each day upon the atoning work of a holy God.

The blood of the animal offered was sprinkled around the altar of the burnt offering reminding us that access to God is always and alone through the blood. It further represented the soul that is poured out in praise and thanksgiving.

Special Instructions

In Leviticus 3:16-17 we note that they were to eat neither fat nor blood. They were not to eat either one because of their peculiar sanctity. Their homes were hereby made a sanctuary. Thus they were to live as redeemed people, realizing their dependence upon God's atoning blood.

According to Leviticus 17:11-12, there are two reasons why blood was not to be eaten. First, in it is the life of the flesh. Second, it is the divinely appointed means of atonement for sin. We are told that *"it shall be a perpetual statute for your generations throughout all your dwellings…"* (Lev. 3:17). Thus it was to be a constant reminder of our dependence upon the blood of God's sacrifice, enabling us to delight in every remembrance of His work. Further, it was to be a reminder of the delight that is ours in separating unto Him that which is the best we have and are. It was to be a reminder of the blessings that are ours in Him.

The priest's portion was the breast and right shoulder of the animal. Both were waved signifying that they were given over to God. This command is carried over into the New Testament as Paul wrote: *"Do ye not know that they which minister about holy things live of the things of the Temple? And they which wait at the altar are partakers with the altar? Even so hath the Lord ordained that they which preach the gospel should live of the gospel."* (I Cor. 9:13, 14).

The Process

The animal was offered and killed by the one offering it. The animal was divided by its parts. The memorial portions were burned. The priest's portions were given and waived. The rest of the animal was returned to the offerer for him to eat with his family. Thus, after the sacrifice was offered, the offerer returned home to prepare a festival meal eaten by his family and friends (Lev. 19:5-8). The offerer was the host. The people participating were the thankful guests fellowshipping with their Father–God. This meal was a clear expression of joy, peace, gratitude, sharing, fellowship and friendship. These are all characteristics of true worship.

Lessons to Be Learned

This sacrifice teaches us that all we are and have belongs to the Lord. The giving of ourselves and the fruit of our labor unto Him is to issue forth in thankful praise. In partaking of our daily food we are to be reminded that atonement by the offering of a life is the ground of acceptance with God and should be the basis for offering grace at every meal. Rejoicing in the acceptance we have through Christ, we are able to have true communion with our fellow worshippers and with God. This thought should also permeate the times when we celebrate together around the Lord's Table (The Lord's Supper) and in the other fellowship dinners of the church body.

The Fifth Principle

Total dedication of possessions and self results in overwhelming joy expressed in thankful praise. The act of public worship at those times when the body of the church comes together should be a time of great joy and thanksgiving in the singing of the hymns, the offering of the prayers and our gifts, and the gathering around the preaching of God's precious word. But it can only be thus as each worshipper comes to the service prepared. He must be redeemed and cleansed having dedicated both his life and his labor in order that he may be prepared to offer true praise and thanksgiving. *"I will go into thy house with burnt offerings: I will pay thee my vows, which my lips have uttered, and my mouth hath spoken."* (Psalm 66:13-14). The psalmist also said: *"Enter into his gates with thanksgiving, and into his courts with praise: be thankful unto him and bless his name. For the Lord is good; his mercy is everlasting; and his truth endureth to all generations."* (Psalm 100: 4-5). This is the response of one who has totally committed his life and all he has unto the Lord.

Do you know Him as your personal Saviour? Are you keeping your sins confessed and thus staying cleansed? Have you committed your life, your time (your purpose for living), and your possessions unto Him? Only so can you truly worship Him with praise and thanksgiving. And only thus will you experience the joy and peace that He so wants to share with you in your daily walk (Psalm 16:11) and put on display to the world through your life.

CHAPTER 7

SELFLESS LOVE

Leviticus 5:14-6:7; 7:1-10

God's love for us is unconditional. As He is the example of what we are to be it is important that we understand that our love, by His grace, is also to be unconditional. Apart from a right relationship with Him this is impossible for us. Unconditional love brings with it responsibility both to God and to our fellow man.

The Trespass Offering

The sixth principle of worship is illustrated by the Trespass Offering. This was a required offering. The essential features of this offering are satisfaction and restitution. The primary characteristic of the offense that necessitated this offering was the invasion or disregard of the property rights of others. This offering was required essentially in cases where the sin was more private and confined to the sinner's knowledge.

The Type of Offenses

There were generally two types of offenses. First, there were offenses against God (Leviticus 5:14-19). This involved acts that defraud God of what is rightfully His. For the Jewish people under the law this involved tithes, first fruits, the first born and anything else under the law that God required of them. We too may defraud God in the matter of the tithe. The tithe has always been, from before the establishment of the law, the standard of what God expected. This is illustrated in Genesis 14: 17-24 when Abram gave to Melchizedek, "priest of the most high God" a tithe of all the spoil he gained in the process of rescuing his nephew, Lot. But the standard for the Christian is even higher. Paul instructed the believers in Corinth to: *"lay by him in store, as God hath prospered him."* (I Corinthians 16:2). The tithe is the starting point. But how God prospers you is the standard from there. As with the Jews under the law, there are many ways that we may defraud God with our time, our talents and our possessions.

The second type of offence described in relation to the Trespass Offering is offenses we may commit against another person (Leviticus 6:1-7). The passages under consideration give us several illustrations: denying a trust; defrauding a business partner; disowning a manifest wrong by claiming that it was not your fault; deceit in commerce; and keeping something found and denying possession of it. Essentially, the offenses related to this offering consisted of invading or disregarding the property rights of another person, man or God. These are offenses committed by one after he has been saved (redeemed). So this, indeed, has a very practical application for us today. Remember, anything that affects our relationship with God affects our ability to truly worship.

There is one other point we need to make here. Both types of offenses are considered an offense against God. After describing the various offenses in Leviticus chapter five we are told that *"It is a trespass offering: he hath certainly trespassed against the Lord."* (Leviticus 5:19). This is reinforced in Leviticus 6:2 where offenses against another person are being described and we are told these are a trespass against the Lord.

The order for offering the Trespass Offering

The first step for the offerer was to confess his guilt for the very specific offense. This involved admission of wrongdoing, thus agreeing with God about the specific offense. Jesus illustrated this when he was attempting to wash the feet of his disciples, an incident recorded for us in John chapter 13. Peter refused to allow Jesus to wash his feet.

Jesus responded to Peter saying: *"He that is washed needeth not save to wash his feet, but is clean every whit: and ye are clean, but not all" (John 13:10).* Jesus told him that his sin (condition) was eternally settled; that eternal life for him was a surety. But it is our sins (acts) that so quickly break our fellowship with God and need often to be dealt with. This is precisely what the Apostle John was talking about when he wrote: *"If we confess our sins, he is faithful and just to forgive us our sins, and to cleanse us from all unrighteousness* ((I John 1:9). It is this confession which involves the confession of particular and known sins that restores our fellowship with God.

The offerer then offered the appropriate offering. What was required was a ram from his flocks. This was the case regardless of the economic status of the offender. It was required that he offer the best that he had denoting again that sin is costly. Further he had to make restitution. He not only was to pay back the principle but he was required to pay an additional twenty percent of valuation. If the offense was against God, it was paid to the priest. If the offense was against another person, it was paid to the one who was defrauded. When this payment was made then the ram could be offered and the offender forgiven.

This offering again demonstrated the costliness of forgiveness. Peter reminded us of the costliness of our sins when he wrote: *"Forasmuch as ye know that ye were not redeemed with corruptible things, as silver and gold, from your vain conversation received by tradition from your fathers; but with the precious blood of Christ (Messiah), as of a lamb without blemish and without spot"* I Peter 1:18- 19). Salvation and cleansing are free to us but it cost God His only Son!

The Offering Process

First, the offering was killed in the place of the burnt offering (cf. Leviticus 7:2a). Then its blood was sprinkled on the side of the altar (cf. Leviticus 7:2b). The richest part of the animal was then burned (cf. Leviticus 7:3-5) as in the peace offering. The rest of the sacrificed animal was then given to the priests for food (cf. Leviticus 7:6). But this was to be eaten only by the male priests and not shared with the families. The priest offering the sacrifice was then allowed to take the hide (Leviticus 7:8).

Lessons to be learned

We are here again reminded that sin is costly. Though our sins are forgiven, the act of the sin sets forces in motion that must run their course as God created a causal order, the principle of which is that for every action there is a reaction. David is a good example. He committed both adultery and murder. God forgave him. But the forces put into play by his sins essentially destroyed his family.

There is a difference between forgiveness and consequences. This is clearly seen in the process outlined in the Trespass Offering. The offerer was required to make restoration with the payment of an additional twenty percent value levy which was to be paid whether the offense was against God or another person.

Thus we see that God holds us responsible for the influence our actions have on others. A good policy is to constantly remember to practice the golden rule. *"And as ye would that men should do to you, do ye also to them likewise."* (Luke 6:31). Jesus illustrated this truth in His judgment of the Pharisees when He said: *"But woe to you scribes and Pharisees, hypocrites! For ye shut up the kingdom of heaven against men: for ye neither go in yourselves, neither suffer ye them that are entering to go in"* (Matthew 23:13). Paul put it this way: *"And through thy knowledge shall the weak brother perish, for whom Christ died? But when ye sin so against the brethren, and wound their weak conscience, ye sin against Christ"* (I Corinthians 8:11-12). We are our brother's keeper.

The Sixth Principle of Worship

The sixth principle of worship is that worship is unbroken as we express selfless love both to God and man. It is important that we become sensitive to the influence we have on those around us. For us to love God unconditionally is not difficult when we focus on all that He has done and is doing for us. And when we start loving Him unconditionally it becomes an easy process to love others as God unconditionally loves us.

To put this principle into operation in our life will draw us more intimately into His presence and worship becomes for us even more of an awesome Journey of faith. To God be the glory!

CHAPTER 8

AWARENESS TO SIN

Leviticus Chapters 11 – 15

Loving God unconditionally becomes the foundation for the rest of the twelve principles of worship. Loving Him unconditionally enables us to put the remaining six principles into practical operation. It gives us the capacity to become aware (sensitive) to the sin that is all around us. The lesson we need here to learn is illustrated in Leviticus chapters eleven through fifteen.

Introduction

The theme of the book of Leviticus, as we have earlier noted, is holiness. It becomes the specific issue in the five chapters which are now before us. *"For I am the LORD your God; ye shall therefore sanctify yourselves, and ye shall be holy; for I am holy: neither shall ye defile yourselves with any manner of creeping thing that creepeth upon the earth. For I am the Lord that bringeth you up out of the land of Egypt, to be your God: ye shall therefore be holy, for I am holy."* (Leviticus 11:44-45). In these verses we are informed how to get close to God: be holy as He is holy. What is also implied is how we are to stay in fellowship with Him: stay holy as He is holy. This involves maintaining a separation from sin.

The subject of these five chapters before us is sin. Chapter eleven reminds us of sin's existence. Chapter twelve discusses the transmission of sin. Chapters thirteen and fourteen demonstrate sin's vileness. Chapter fifteen illustrates how sin deforms.

Five Areas of Life Mentioned

There are five areas here mentioned that teach us about sin. The first is food mentioned in Leviticus 11:2-23, 29-30, 41-47. The lesson to be learned through food is to be sensitive to sin and thus choose that which is good. The second issue is death mentioned in Leviticus 11:24-25, 27- 28, 31-40. Through the reality of death we are to understand that sin, which defiles, is really all about us. The third area is in the matter of childbirth where we are reminded to remember that we are born with a sin nature inherited from Adam.

The fourth area mentioned is disease and is found in chapters thirteen and fourteen. Here we are reminded that disease is the result of original sin, the result of the curse brought upon Adam because of his sin. The fifth area deals with personal issues where we are reminded that our flesh is hopelessly defiled, thus in need of continuous cleansing.

Food

The issue related to food is the matter of what is clean and what is unclean. God's intent was more than using this to set Israel apart as a unique people who were His. Because of the culture of the time there were certain foods that could be unhealthy. Because God cares He instructed them to stay away from those foods. This was the practical reason. But with God there is always in everything He does a spiritual lesson to be learned. Here the lesson is that His people needed to develop a sensitivity (awareness) to sin. Sin is defined in the Bible in at least two ways. In I John 3:4 sin is defined as the breaking of the law. *"Whosoever committeth sin transgresseth also the law: for sin is the transgression of the law."* The broader definition which includes the one already given is found in Deuteronomy 9:7. *"Remember, and forget not, how thou provokedst the LORD thy God to wrath in the wilderness: from the day that thou didst depart out of the land of Egypt, until ye came unto this place, ye have been rebellious against the LORD."* Breaking of

God's clearly stated law is simply, on our part, rebellion against Him. So sin, simply, may be defined as rebellion against God whether it is in thought, word or deed.

In the illustration God used the basis of the distinction as to that which was carnivorous or a scavenger making all else clean. The practical purpose was the preservation of good health. But it also was intended to make Israel separate from the nations around them (cf. Deuteronomy 14:2).

God's further purpose was to infuse the mind of Israel with moral distinctions, a purpose so clearly stated in Leviticus 11:44-45 which we read at the beginning of this chapter. That all of this relates to us today is made clear in the incident relating to Peter found in Acts 10:12-15.

God's purpose for Israel was that they should share the revelation of God's love and grace with the entire world.

Because they did not, He set Israel (the nation) aside so that the gospel could be proclaimed to Gentiles with a very specific purpose relating back to the Jew. Note what Paul said: *"I say then, Have they stumbled that they should fall? God forbid: but rather through their fall salvation is come unto the Gentiles, **for to provoke them to jealousy**"* (Romans 11:11). How do we provoke another, Jew or Gentile, to jealousy? Is it not that they see our life as so different and blessed that they want what we have found?

There is a very real need for us who are today His family to also develop an awareness to sin as we, too, are described as a unique people who, by our very living are set apart from the sinful world. Peter stated it this way: *"But ye are a chosen generation, a royal priesthood, a holy nation, a peculiar people; that ye should show forth the praises of him who hath called you out of darkness into his marvelous light."* In Titus 2:13-14 Paul wrote: *"Looking for that blessed hope, and the glorious appearing of the great God and our Saviour Jesus Christ; who gave Himself for us, that He might redeem us from all iniquity, and purify unto himself a peculiar people, zealous of good works."* So we need to develop an awareness of sin in order that we might discern what defiles and consciously choose not to be defiled.

Death

Death was a reminder of the curse from the fall. *"The wages of sin is death."* (Romans 6:23a). The moment that Adam sinned he both died and began to die. Death defined is separation. Spiritual death is separation from God. Spiritual death occurred immediately after Adam sinned. This was seen when both Adam and Eve hid in the garden when God came to commune with them. Physical death occurs with the separation of the soul and spirit from the body. The process of physical death began the moment Adam sinned.

But death also defiles (cf. Leviticus 11:32-35). The things defiled in this list are normal household items teaching us two things. First, Cleanliness is taught. There should be nothing in our home that either defiles or is defiled. Something in our home that would defile could be a picture that draws out our old nature or anything else that would draw us away from serving the Lord and back toward the world. At least two items that could draw us either way is the television set and the computer. It may be defiled or clean depending on how it is used and how we view it.

This also teaches us that our daily private walk needs to be kept undefiled even in the privacy of our own home. The key is attitude. Consider when we are dressing. When we choose what we will wear each day or for special occasions what is our motive, pride or humility; pumping the flesh or honoring God? You see, even in what we might consider trifling matters we need to be reminded that whatever we do we are to do it all to God's glory.

Washing reminds us of the need for cleanliness and separation from things that defile. Paul was focusing on this emphasis when he wrote: *"For this ye know, that no whoremonger, nor unclean person, nor covetous man, who is an idolater, hath any inheritance in the kingdom of Christ and of God. Let no man deceive you with any vain words: for because of these things cometh the wrath of God upon the children of disobedience. Be not ye therefore partakers with them."* (Ephesians 5:5-7). We need to become aware of even these small things that could defile.

Childbirth

Childbirth speaks of the transmission of the sin nature, the propagation of the original sin. It is a reminder that the woman has brought another sinner into the world. *"Behold, I was shapen in iniquity; and in sin did my mother conceive me."* (Psalm 51:5). In Job 25:4 it is put this way: *"How then can man be justified with God? Or how can he be clean that is born of a woman?"* It was Paul who wrote that we were: *"by nature the children of wrath, even as others."* (Ephesians 2:3c). The time of purification was to be a reminder of her part in the transmission of sin. Even in this, Israel, as an elect people, were to learn the meaning of true separation, experiencing in daily life the difference between the holy and the profane.

Disease

In chapters thirteen and fourteen the issue is leprosy. But this is not leprosy as we today understand it. These are simply diseases of the skin. Though leprosy is a type of sin, this passage does not suggest that disease comes to a person because he has sinned. However, it may be a type of indwelling sin which must be dealt with before we can continue to have fellowship with God, that is, to worship. The message of these chapters is to point out that the holy God requires that our very garments and homes are to be holy.

Personal

The issues specified here are all related to the process of reproduction. Charles Erdman, in his exposition of Leviticus 15 stated: "The necessity of their cleansing was an implication that the very sources of life have been affected by sin."[xi]

Andrew Bonar stated: "The secret uncleanness, known only to the person's self, represents the secret sins, or the secret, quiet oozing out of sin from the natural heart – its flow of pollution while not a word is spoken, not an act done, not a motion visible to the eye of our fellow-men."[xii] Here we are reminded of the subtle nature of how the sin nature within us might seep out. We must be constantly aware that in the flesh we are hopelessly defiled. It leaves us nothing in which to glory. This reveals the need for continual cleansing, the washing of water which is the word of God.

Remember, the issue here is becoming aware of the sin about us that we might recognize its subtle attacks. Only if we are aware of how sin works can we be prepared to implement the tools God gives us through His word and His indwelling Holy Spirit enabling us to stay in fellowship with our wonderful Creator and God, thus worshipping. The amazing truth is that the closer we walk with God the more aware we become of sin for He is holy and His holiness that embraces us heightens our awareness.

Seventh Principle of Worship

We must be constantly aware of our depraved nature and the defilement of sin all around us. Awareness to sin is necessary to identify it and then enabling us to avail ourselves of the means of God's grace provided to overcome sin. As we learn to do this through His word and the power of the indwelling Holy Spirit our worship relationship with God can continue to grow and deepen. This really is not difficult when all of the other principles that precede this one are in place and actively functioning. You see, worship truly is an awesome journey of faith!

PART III

THE CHARACTER OF WORSHIP

CHAPTER 9

PREPARATION

Leviticus Chapters 8-9

Thus far in this awesome journey of faith we have learned that it begins when we recognize our personal need and by faith seeing Jesus, the Christ, as the only viable answer to our need, we receive Him as our Redeemer. Having received Him placed us in a worship relationship with God our Creator. We quickly learned that sin breaks fellowship, leading us to see the necessity to keep a short account of our sins in order to have an ongoing worship experience with our Creator. Love for God through His Son now has become the motivating, driving factor in our life leading us to both dedicate our life and labor unto Him. This causes us to recognize that any good in us is of Him leading us to offer Him thanksgiving and joyous praise. By now we have come to the realization that God has only our best interest at heart. We now see that His love is unconditional, selfless, creating within us the desire to also love unconditionally. But sin is so subtle and continues to be a problem leading us to recognize our need to become more aware of sin, how it beguiles and snares us with its seemingly innocuous traps. Only as we develop, by God's grace, an awareness of the sin that is all around us can we continue to grow in our worship relationship with our Creator.

Having come this far in our journey we now begin to learn the importance of consecrated service as the next step in understanding the worship experience as an awesome journey of faith. The importance of this step is taught us in Leviticus chapters eight and nine. The example God uses is the Levitical priesthood. In this chapter we will discuss the first of three principles of worship that are related to the priesthood.

There are two reasons why the study of the Levitical priesthood is important. First, the Bible teaches that all true believers are priests. Note what God said to Moses: *"And ye shall be unto me a kingdom of priests, and a holy nation."* (Exodus 19:6a). The apostle Peter reinforced this as it relates to believers in the Church Age. *"But ye are a chosen generation, a royal priesthood, a holy nation, a peculiar people; that ye should show forth the praises of him who hath called you out of darkness into his marvelous light."* (I Peter 2:9). So a true believer is a priest.

Also, according to Hebrews 3:1 and 4:14, Jesus the Messiah is our High Priest. *"Wherefore, holy brethren, partakers of the heavenly calling, consider the Apostle and High Priest of our profession, Christ (Messiah) Jesus."* Again we read: *"Seeing then that we have a great high priest, that is passed into the heavens, Jesus the Son of God, let us hold fast our profession."* The Levitical Priests were dependent upon their relationship to Aaron. So, today the believer's priesthood is dependent upon his relationship to Messiah Jesus (cf. Revelation 7:9-17).

Preparation for the Priesthood

In his preparation for the priesthood three things are done to the priest. First, he is washed (cf. Leviticus 8:6). Washing, as we have already seen, symbolizes regeneration (cf. Titus 3:5; Revelation 7:14; Hebrews 10:22). Secondly, the priest is clothed (cf. Leviticus 8:13). This symbolizes holiness (cf. Revelation 3:5). Then he was anointed (cf. Leviticus 8:30). This symbolizes the giving of the Holy Spirit for service (cf. Acts 4:31; I Corinthians 2:4-5).

There were two features that distinguished the High Priest from all of the other priests. First, The High Priest was anointed <u>before</u> the slaying of the consecration sacrifice (cf. Leviticus 8:12-14). This typified Messiah, the sinless one, who required no preparation for His anointing of the Holy Spirit.

Secondly, the anointing oil was poured <u>only</u> upon the High Priest. This typifies the fullness of the Spirit upon Messiah Jesus. Notice what the Apostle John had to say about this matter: *"For he whom God hath sent speaketh the words of God: for God giveth not the Spirit by measure unto him"* (John 3:34). If you go back and look at the context of this verse you will see that he was speaking of Jesus. This is also the message the writer of Hebrews was teaching in Hebrews 1:1-9. Notice what he wrote of Jesus in verse nine: *"Thou hast loved righteousness, and hated iniquity; therefore God, even thy God, hath anointed thee with the oil of gladness above thy fellows."*

The Order of the Sacrifices

Notice the order of the required sacrifices. First sin had to be expiated (Leviticus 8:14-17) through the sin offering which required a bullock upon whom was placed the priest's sins through the laying on of his hands symbolizing the transference of sin from the priest to the bullock which was then slain with its blood sprinkled about the altar to make reconciliation. Even here we see the necessity of the exchange of life principle. Thus this was to be a reminder of their human weaknesses. This was followed by the burnt offering which was totally consumed depicting the total dedication of life to God. Then this act was followed by the trespass offering as seen in chapter eight verses 22 to 24. The blood in this case was sprinkled upon the ears of the priest signifying a call for proper hearing of God's directions and obedience. The blood applied upon the thumbs signified a call for approved service. Even one's hands are to be consecrated to God's service. Finally the blood was also placed upon the toes signifying a call for a holy walk. All of this symbolized the importance of one's whole being consecrated unto God for His service. Paul, speaking of this very issue, wrote: *"I beseech you therefore, brethren, by the mercies of God, that ye present your bodies a living sacrifice, holy, acceptable unto God, which is your reasonable service."* (Romans 12:1). Charles Erdman described this ritual thusly: "Thus it was indicated that in view of the blood which has been shed, one who is truly serving God must be ready to hear His word, to undertake His work, and to run at His command."[xiii]

The Order of the Events

The events followed a clear and logical order. Sin was expiated. Consecration was completed. Installation into service was demonstrated. And service was begun (Leviticus 9:9-21). In the next verse (v 22) the new priests blessed the people. Aaron and Moses retired into the Tabernacle and then returned. This symbolized the Messiah, the Prophet-Priest, who came to bless the people, returned to the heavenly tabernacle, but who is coming again. Upon returning, they again blessed the people, and God's glory fell, consuming the sacrifice and causing the people to draw near and worship. When Messiah Jesus returns, God's glory will be manifest, and every knee shall bow and every tongue confess that Messiah Jesus is Lord to the glory of God the father.

Lessons to Be Learned

We are to understand that our priesthood is for the benefit of others, not others for the benefit of our priesthood. We are to serve God to be a blessing to others, always viewing others as better than ourselves. Only when we have put the earlier principles of worship into practice can we find the love that enables us to honestly do this. We also need to understand that all we do is to be a consecrated service unto the Lord. To view all that we do from this perspective will transform our life and our relationships with others.

As Moses and Aaron departed and returned bringing God's great glory with them, so our High Priest, under whom we labor, who has come and departed, will also come again, imparting God's glory to us and to all mankind. *"And every man that hath this hope in him purifieth himself, even as he is pure."* (I John 3:3). This will cause our service to result in others seeing Christ at work in our lives and be moved in their heart to also desire to worship the King of Kings and Lord of Lords.

Eighth Principle of Worship

We are not prepared until we understand that we are priests unto God by which our service (our life) is totally consecrated unto Him. Remember the words of Paul found in Ephesians 2:10. *"For we are his workmanship, created in Christ Jesus unto good works, which God hath before ordained that we should walk in them."*

This leads us to the next principle of worship that is also related to our priesthood. Let us first begin making application of this principle. Then let us go on as we move forward in this awesome journey of faith.

CHAPTER 10

PERCEPTION

Leviticus Chapters 10, 21, 22

In the previous chapter we began our study of the character of worship. In this study we are taking a look at Israel's priesthood as we develop three further principles of worship. The first lesson taught us by the priesthood of Israel is the importance, nay, the necessity of consecrated service. This leads us to the ninth principle of worship exemplified by the priesthood which is the necessity for a proper perception. This perception becomes clear as we examine the responsibilities of the priesthood as laid out by God through Moses to Aaron. As we move forward in this study let us again be reminded that in the Christian economy all believers are priests. We shall consider four areas of responsibility.

Careful Observance of God's Word

The first area of responsibility for a priest is demonstrated by the incident with Nadab and Abihu recorded in Leviticus 10: 1-7. Remember, both were now consecrated into the priesthood. Yet, for whatever their reason, they took their censors, created and offered strange fire before the Lord which had not been commanded.

Their sin was that they took it upon themselves to step beyond God's clear instructions. They took their censors without God's instruction and, rather than taking fire from off the altar, they kindled their own fire. Then they sprinkled incense upon the fire and offered it up to God. The fire on the altar signified God's consuming holiness. The incense symbolized the prayers of the saints. When the two were properly joined the fire of God's holiness consumed the prayers of the saints creating a sweet smelling savor of those prayers unto God.

In a sense Abraham and Sarah did the same thing under different circumstances. God had promised them a child. They were beyond the normal time for childbearing. So they decided that they would help God fulfill His promise. Their action, in stepping beyond God's will, resulted in a sin for which Israel and the Jewish people are still experiencing consequences. There continues to this day a conflict between the seed of Ishmael and Isaac in the present Middle East conflict between Israel and the Arab and Palestinian people.

Because this was a public sin the judgment was public. God's holiness, which was publically transgressed, reached out and consumed them and *"they died before the Lord."* Was not the sin of Ananias and Sapphira similar with the same result as recorded in Act 5: 1-11?

This has a warning for those who would introduce worldly music and other practices supposedly aimed to attract more people to attend public worship. Many pastors have softened their message preaching a "more positive" gospel so that those who would attend could feel more comfortable. Basil Atkinson stated the lesson here to be learned as it relates to public worship. He wrote: "This incident provides a serious warning against introducing anything of man into Christian worship, doctrine or practice."[xiv]

But let us as individuals also remember, we are sanctified that we may live and walk in His presence (cf. Leviticus 10:3). So we are reminded that God's plans are perfect and need no tweaking from us. And that includes the acts of public worship. To walk in His presence is to walk carefully according to His word both privately and publicly.

Careful focus on our Purpose

The second area of responsibility we are directed to consider is the area of strong drink (cf. vv 9-11). Here we have a prohibition for using strong drink. It is important to note that this prohibition related only to when they were ministering in the Tabernacle. The text states: *"Do not drink wine nor strong drink; thou, nor thy sons with thee, when ye go into the tabernacle of the congregation"* (v.9). The phrase, "when ye go into", creates a condition. This may well typify intoxication or obsession with the pleasures or cares of this present world. Jesus, when he shared with His disciples the parable of the sower as recorded in Luke 8:14, stated: *"and that which fell among thorns are they, which, when they have heard, go forth, and are choked with cares and riches and pleasures of this life, and bring no fruit to perfection."* Anything that intoxicates or becomes for us an obsession is to be avoided. These may be things that, in and of themselves, are not sinful. But we are to avoid them because we are called to be wholly engaged in serving God.

We are informed that this is a serious matter as is made clear in the potential result: *"Lest ye die."* Worldliness and carnality are inconsistent with holiness. We are called to be holy.

Beyond the risk of judgment we are given two further reasons why we should take this matter seriously. In verse ten we are told that we need a clear and focused mind to distinguish between that which is holy and that which is unholy. This is certainly needful for us to make right choices. In verse eleven we are reminded of the need of a clear mind to fulfill our responsibility of teaching others the statutes and principles of a godly life. And remember, much more of our teaching is done by example than by formal teaching in a classroom setting. This, indeed, is a serious matter.

Careful Love for our Saviour

In verses 12 through 15 Moses spoke to Aaron and his remaining sons of the high privilege of serving in the priestly office and their entitlement to certain portions of the food offered as sacrifices. When he discovered that on this day they had burnt everything, even their food portion, Moses chided them for their disobedience in this matter. Note Aaron's response: "And Aaron said unto Moses, Behold, this day have they offered their sin offering and their burnt *offering before the LORD; and such things have befallen me: and if I had eaten of the sin offering today, should it be accepted in the sight of the LORD?"* (v.19). Aaron pointed out that his sons had offered the sin sacrifice and burnt offering. But before it was completed they sinned thus interrupting the completion of the process. Could, then, the sin sacrifice have been acceptable unto God? And would he (Aaron) not have sinned had he partaken of it? In verse twenty we see that Moses recognized that Aaron had entered into the spirit and meaning of the rites and accepted Aaron's response as correct.

The lesson taught here is that serving the Lord is not to be a formality or legalistic activity. Our worship and service are to be Spirit oriented and motivated out of our love for God, never an act of doing right because it is right to do. In I Corinthians 3:11-15 Paul raises the same issue for the believer who will stand one day at the Bema Seat to be judged for his deeds. In verse thirteen Paul wrote: *"And the fire shall try every man's work of what sort it is."* The Greek word is "hopoios" which literally means "quality". Thus it is not so much the deed as the motive behind it that matters. Jesus, Himself, speaks to this issue in John 14:15-24. Four times, in four different ways, Jesus teaches that what really matters when it comes to serving Him is our "love for Him." Four times He uses "agapao" which is "unconditional love." The letter of the law does matter. But it is superseded by the spirit of the law. Thus does ritual yield to reality.

Careful Maintenance of our testimony

When we have an opportunity to witness the gospel to another we need to recognize that the first gospel a lost person is going to read is the gospel according to our life. Leviticus chapters twenty-one and twenty-two contain instructions for the priests that are intended to preserve their holiness. All of the issues herein dealt with are typical and fall into four areas: personal appearance, marriage, family, and service.

The instructions for personal appearance are given to us in verse five. *"They shall not make baldness upon their head, neither shall they shave off the corner of their beard, nor make any cuttings in their flesh."* The Jewish priests were not to do anything that would imitate the signs of mourning among the heathen peoples of the Middle East (cf. Leviticus 19:27-28). Cutting off the hair, shaving the beard and tattooing were heathen mourning customs. Thus we are instructed that we are to be careful not to give the appearance of the worldly. Today, in our worldly culture, for a man to wear long hair and thus appear as a woman is a sign of rebellion. In the broader sense, we are admonished to dress modestly or in a manner that does not emphasize the physical body. Tattooing today is still a worldly issue that emphasizes the flesh. In our personal appearance we are called to emphasize the holiness of the one who has bought and called us into His service.

A priest was not to marry an unchaste or divorced woman (cf. vv. 7, 14). The word "profane" denotes defiled or polluted. Thus the issue here is one of holiness. God has always had a higher standard for those who would lead His people. They are, of course, to lead by example and be above reproach.

It is significant that both Jesus and the apostle Paul recognized marriage as a sacred picture of the holy and loving relationship between Christ and His church (cf. John 14:1-3; Ephesians 5:28-33). Peter also reminds all New Covenant believers that we are to be *a royal priesthood, a holy nation, a peculiar people; that ye should show forth the praises of him who hath called you out of darkness into his marvelous light"* (I Peter 2:9). Thus, like the Old Covenant priests, we are called *"to show forth (His) praises"* in all things, including the marriage relationship.

Even our service must be kept holy unto Him (cf. Leviticus 22:1-2; 6-7). What an important reminder, that it is essential for us to begin each day in prayer (talking with Him) and Bible reading (allowing Him to talk with us) committing our life afresh into His hands and walking carefully in His presence lest we be profaned.

There are five different words translated "worship" in the New Testament. Each word is different. The first word, found in Luke 14:10, literally means "esteem". This is a call for us to give God the first and highest place in our life. The second word is found in Acts 17:23 and literally means "to reverence". Again, only God is worthy of our reverence. To revere is to show one the deepest respect, love and awe.

The third word translated worship is found in Acts 17:25 and literally means "to serve". It means to serve one with respect, love and awe. The fourth word translated worship, found in Colossians 2:18, literally means "to kiss the hand." This is an act of love and devotion for one who has done something for us. There is a fifth word translated "worship" in the New Testament which denotes public worship and is so used in Acts 24:14; Philippians 3:3; and Hebrews 10:2.

Put all of these words together and we see that worship is not going to a place, or bowing the knee. It is not the act of prostrating ourselves before another, nor offering a candle or burning incense. Worship is all of the heart. It is the love of the heart that esteems God supremely, that loves Him passionately, that leads one to reverence that name above every name, and from morning to night do all in your power, by His grace, just to live for Him. Again, we see that worship is not just an act. It is a life. This was the lesson God was seeking to teach to the priests of Israel.

The Ninth Principle of Worship

The ninth principle of worship is that careful obedience to God's word is the essential perception in maintaining a worship relationship with our Creator and Redeemer. James stated the principle a bit differently. He wrote: *"Be ye doers of the word, and not hearers only, deceiving your own selves. For if any be a hearer of the word, and not a doer, he is like unto a man beholding his natural face in a glass: for he beholdeth himself, and goeth his way, and straightway forgetteth what manner of man he was. But whoso looketh into the perfect law of liberty, and continueth therein, he being not a forgetful hearer, but a doer of the work, this man shall be blessed in his deed."* (James 1:22-25).

The important issue to remember here is that all of this is impossible to us unless we have put into place the first eight principles of worship. Each principle activated makes the next principle doable. Truly this is an awesome journey of faith! Are you ready for the next step? I know. The air is beginning to get thin. But the next principle is a principle of encouragement.

CHAPTER 11

PROVISION

Leviticus 6:16-18; 7:6-10, 14, 31-36

We have considered the preparation for the priesthood and the perspective that enables our priesthood to be successful. In this chapter we shall discuss God's provision for the priesthood. The essential truth here is that the provision for a successful priesthood comes directly from God Himself.

As He does not want us to fail, He has promised to give us everything we need to be successful. Jesus Himself addresses this very important issue in His final resurrection appearance recorded for us in Acts 1:6-8. Notice that before He gives His followers their marching orders He said: *"But ye shall receive power…"* The Greek word used here is *"dunamis"* which is the root word for dynamite. It is used seventy-five times in the New Testament, always in relation to either God, Jesus (Christ), or the Holy Spirit. It literally means power, might or ability. The power or ability to fulfill Christ's commission was given us with the gift of the indwelling Holy Spirit. Again, notice what Jesus said: *"But ye shall receive power after that the Holy Spirit is come upon you."* The point is that God never calls us to do anything except that He empowers (enables) us to do it. Notice, Jesus does not command us to do anything until after we are empowered by the indwelling Holy

Spirit, a gift that is given the moment we believe (cf. Romans 8:9; I Corinthians 3:16). So we are without excuse.

Many years ago, when we had started a storefront church in SE Baltimore, we were getting things together for our summer Vacation Bible School. We were a small church running around forty at the time. I had everything together except for someone to teach the mission lessons each day. I had had the privilege of leading a dear lady to the Lord, baptizing and discipling her. She was an excited new believer who was anxious to serve. After she was saved she said to me: "Pastor, I will do anything but just do not ask me to teach." As I prayed for God's choice to assume this opportunity I was led to Pat. When I told God she would not do it He told me that she was His choice. So I made an appointment with her to ask her if she would join me in praying for a matter. I knew that she would. I told her that I wanted God's choice for this teaching position and I needed someone to pray with me for one week, that God would confirm His choice both to her and to me. Then I would know who to ask. She agreed. Next week, as we had agreed, I visited her to discuss the matter. I asked if God had spoken to her on the matter and she told me that He had. So I asked whom God had shown her to be His choice. She told me that it was she, and I agreed. She said that she just could not do it. It was then that I asked her if God would ever ask someone to do anything they could not do with His help. She said: "no". With great fear she agreed to trust the Lord for His enablement. When the first day of VBS was finished Pat was ecstatic! She had found God faithful and became one of our best teachers.

Regarding the various offerings given by God through Moses to the priests, we are encouraged by the fact that God has promised to provide for all our needs. We will look at just four of the offerings.

The Meal Offering

With every offering that the people were to offer God made a provision for the needs of the priests. The meal offering was divided into two portions, a handful for the Lord and the remainder for the priests. Remember, everything that God instructed to be done in the religious practices of His people was for the purpose of teaching the people a truth. The meal offering was divided into two portions to typify the two aspects of Christ's sacrifice, the one directed toward God and the other toward man. First, Jesus offered Himself to do the will of God to bring Him satisfaction for sin (cf. John 6:38; Romans 3:25; I John 2:2). In the same act He brought salvation to His people. So the emphasis of the meal offering is communion. The point is that both God and we who have believed are satisfied in Christ. The significance here is that we feast on that which satisfies God's heart and that it also more than satisfies us. This is the great truth of the meal offering. The fact that the priests were instructed to partake of their portion in a holy place indicates that God and redeemed man are sitting together at the same table feasting upon Christ. What does this bring to us right now? David stated it well in Psalm 16:11b: *"In thy presence is fullness of joy; and at thy right hand there are pleasures for evermore."* As we learn to fellowship with God we find complete satisfaction: "fullness of joy" and *"pleasures for evermore."* What a provision! No reason to fear. No reason to worry. Just complete satisfaction.

The Sin Offering

According to Leviticus 6:25-26, the sin offering was killed in the same place where the burnt offering was killed. Then, it was given as food to the priest that offered it as a sin offering.

It is important for us to understand that there were two different sin offerings. The first sin offering was killed and completely burned. This typified the complete sacrifice of Jesus on the cross. The sin offering mentioned here was offered by one who already had received the benefit of the first sin offering removing sin from him thus making him acceptable to God. To help us better understand the relationship between the two sin offerings God instructed that the sin offering here mentioned was to be killed in the same place as was the burnt offering. So they are related. The first offering which was killed, offered and burnt, typified Christ's sacrifice at Calvary providing us with the means of redemption. The significance of the second sin offering was to remind us that Jesus, as the sin offering, was always to benefit his people in their practical daily living. John stated this thought well: *"My little children, these things write I unto you, that ye sin not. And if any man sin, we have an advocate with the Father, Jesus Christ the righteous:*

and He is the propitiation for our sins…" (I John 2:1-2a). His offering was for all sin, past, present and future.

Notice that in the first sin offering the issue is "our sin." But in this sin offering the issue is "our sins." God has a provision for us even when we sin after having been saved. John gives us a picture of a court scene with God as the judge, Satan as the accuser, and Jesus as the defense attorney. Satan justly accuses us. God's gavel begins to lower as He prepares to pronounce us guilty. But Christ, not defending our wrongdoing, simply states: "But Father, I died for that sin." And we are forgiven based on His shed blood.

Some would say that this idea gives us license to sin. That just is not true. When we were saved our heart was changed. Our desire, after being redeemed, is to live pleasing unto Him. He takes away our desire to sin. Because He first loved us we now are moved to love Him. Yet, sin is so subtle. And sometimes we just do it without really understanding at the moment that it is sin. Fellowship is broken. But, when we realize that fellowship is broken and we begin to look back to find the reason, God has provided us with the means to be re-instated. *"If we confess our sins, he is faithful and just to forgive us our sins, and to cleanse us from all unrighteousness."* (I John 1:9). The sin must be known and confessed. The issue here is the maintenance of fellowship with God in the course of our daily living. This is the significance of the sin offering as it demonstrates God's provision to meet the ongoing need to deal with potential sins. How great is His love!

The Burnt Offering

The key verse here is Leviticus 7:8 which informs us that the priest who offers a burnt offering is allowed to take the hide from off the animal and use it as he wishes. In that economy this was very valuable. It was most often used to make clothing, blankets, etc. Selling it would bring the means to care for other needs. We are thus shown that God has made provision for all of our needs. But notice this was a gift only to those who serve Him. The message is clear. If we will serve God with a full heart He will take care of our every need. So, you see, God has promised everything we need to be successful in our worship, an awesome journey of faith.

When we were still young believers, God led us to pioneer a church in inner city Baltimore. In those days we knew nothing about "faith" missions. We did not search out a mission agency that was willing to endorse and send us. God called us to go do it and so we went honestly giving no thought as to how we would take care of our needs. He miraculously provided us with free housing. Then He enabled us to purchase a house getting a loan though I had no visible source of income.

We lived, in those days, from meal to meal. In mid- November of that first year, while working in my office, I received a call from a dear lady who asked me how things were going. I told her: "great". She responded: "You always say that. I will call your wife." And that is what she did. She asked Joyce very specific questions about what was in the pantry, etc. That afternoon, when I came home, I found two large boxes on our porch filled with all kinds of groceries. We brought them into the house and, weeping, gave thanks to God. It was then that we decided to split the gift evenly with another missionary family with two small children who were in the same need as we, even though we could have used them all.

For the next five weeks or so, though we never shared our need with anyone except God, food kept showing up on our doorstep and we kept sharing it with others who we knew were in need. This continued until the day before Christmas when we learned of a family in our church neighborhood who had been robbed. We again put together another box, enough to feed that needy family for one week until he got another paycheck, and took the food to them. When we arrived home after the delivery, we found one more box of groceries! What a great Christmas that was! But the important thing was that God taught us that if we would faithfully serve and honor Him He would take care of us. That was almost forty years ago. He has never failed us all these ensuing years, as undeserving as we are. We experienced God's faithful provision. So can you.

The Peace Offering

Please read Leviticus 7:14, 31-36. The specific provision offered to God's servants in the burnt offering was clothing and a source of income. The provision that He promises here is food. Through their serving the needs of the priests were cared for by God's provision. The message to us is that, if we will faithfully serve Him, He will take care of us.

The Tenth Principle of Worship

The tenth principle simply stated is God's blessings are bestowed upon us when we are in a right relationship with Him.

Notice the order God has established. If we will believe, He will redeem us. Having been redeemed, if we will do what is necessary to keep a short sin account with Him, we can fellowship with Him and He will fellowship with us. If then we will dedicate our life and labor unto Him that will lead us to be thankful giving us the desire to praise Him. Our love for Him then continues to grow and becomes selfless, giving us a deeper awareness to sin and its wiles. This leads us to consecrated (God blessed) service, necessitating that we walk in careful obedience which results in Him encouraging us by providing for our every need.

Remember, that worship, if we get it into proper perspective, is an awesome journey. It is not a simple act or deed now and then but a life that begins the day we were saved and is ultimately concluded when we enter fully into His presence. But wait! That is not all. There are still two more principles before we make a final application. Are you ready? Let's continue this awesome journey of faith.

PART IV

WALKING IN WORSHIP

CHAPTER 12

PERSONAL SANCTIFICATION

LEVITICUS 17 -20

In our study thus far we have considered the foundation for worship, the attitude of worship and the character of worship. In the process of this study we have discovered ten principles of worship. We have noted that these principles are like an inverse pyramid. Each succeeding principle cannot become operative in one's life until the preceding principles are functioning because they provide what is necessary for us to implement the next principle.

Are you beginning to see that this awesome journey of faith becomes easier each time we master a principle and move on to the next? Some years back I had the privilege of leading a Jewish man to his Messiah. I told him that the walk with his Lord would become easier in time. He continued in our weekly Bible study and almost every week for two years would ask: "When will it become easier?" Then one night when he came to the study he was just radiating. I asked him what was happening. He said: "You were right. It does get easier!"

All that we have been learning through this study is based upon the only book in the Bible that can be considered to be the believer's handbook for worship: the book of Leviticus. In this section of our study titled "Walking in Worship", which is now before us, we will develop the final two principles and then add some thoughts regarding the role of public worship in the believer's life.

Understanding Sanctification

Before we can move forward in this study we must have an understanding of what is meant by sanctification. The word "sanctify" is used one hundred and six times in the Old Testament and thirty-one times in the New Testament. It means "to be set apart." It deals with matters of position and relationship. In the Bible sense, as it relates to humans, it signifies that a person is separated from that which is unholy and brought into a position and relationship with God who is holy. Sanctification implies holiness for only that which is holy can stand in the presence of the one and only Holy God.

At this point we need to understand two things. First it does not mean nor does it imply sinless perfection. Sinless perfection teaches that one is brought into a holy relationship with God and therefore can no longer sin. However, we can live without sinning only in so far as we maintain a totally yielded relationship with our Lord which necessitates a moment by moment choice on our part to claim the victory He, by His grace, provides to us. As we have already learned, God gives us everything we need to defeat temptation. But temptation is only defeated as we by faith apply those divine provisions in our daily walk. Sanctification does not imply sinless perfection.

As one studies the biblical concept of sanctification he is quick to discover that it is progressive. The Bible repeatedly calls the believer to greater heights. Notice what Paul wrote to the Corinthians: *"Now the Lord is that Spirit: and where the Spirit of the Lord is, there is liberty. But we all, with open face beholding as in a glass the glory of the Lord, are changed into the same image from glory to glory even as by the Spirit of the Lord."* (II Corinthians 3:17-18). Notice that this is a process. This is *"from glory to glory"* as the Spirit conforms the true believer into the very image of Christ. Dr. J. H. Bernard, in The Expositor's Greek Testament wrote: "All Christian believers are transformed into the same image of Christ, from glory to glory (i.e. progressively). Our progress in glory is continuous, as becomes the work of the Spirit from whom it springs (John 16:14; Romans 8:11)."[xv] Sanctification thus speaks of an awesome journey of faith.

Also, we are to understand that from the biblical standpoint there are two aspects to sanctification in the believer: positional sanctification and experimental sanctification. Positional sanctification occurs the moment we believe for it is at that point of the new birth experience that our sins are forgiven and we are brought into God's glorious presence. This position has no relationship to the new believer's daily walk except that it should motivate him to a holy walk. Only as we understand this does the many calls to the believer to walk holy make any sense (cf. Romans 12:1-2; Ephesians 4:1; Colossians 3:1). In the Romans 12 passage Paul uses the Greek word *"metamorphoo"* which means to be changed from one form to another, as in a caterpillar worm becoming a monarch butterfly. In this process old things pass away, behold all things become new. We have been accepted in the Beloved so we are not righteous in ourselves but in Him. Positional sanctification is as perfect as Christ is perfect. In our position in Christ, the believer stands righteous and accepted before God forever. We are a new creature. This is his position the moment he believes and is saved.

The rest of our life is spent learning to apply that sanctification to our daily walk by God's grace. This is experimental or personal sanctification. It is dependent upon the degree of our yieldedness to God which results in our separation from sin and in our spiritual growth. This is the essence of Paul's teaching found in Romans 6:1-14. Notice the words "should", "Knowing", "Reckon", "let not", "neither yield", "but yield". These all demand responsibility and action on our part. The purpose of this chapter is to help us realize that victory in the realm of experimental sanctification may be realized only as it is claimed by faith and the conditions for a Holy Spirit-filled life are met. Such victory should be ever increasing as the believer comes to know his own helplessness and the access he has to God's marvelous power. Yes, the walk becomes easier each time we, by faith, access His power. If you have applied the truths and activated the principles thus far shared in this study you should already be well on your way in this awesome journey of faith.

Moses, in Leviticus chapters seventeen to twenty, addresses this matter of sanctification. In chapter seventeen he deals with ecclesiastical sanctification. In the following two chapters Moses discusses the issues of personal sanctification. All of this relates to the matter of personal sanctification.

Ecclesiastical Sanctification

First, Moses lays out God's instructions on the issue of ecclesiastical sanctification. The word "ecclesiastical" comes from the Greek root word *ecclesia* which speaks of a called out assembly. The comparable Hebrew term is *kahal* and is used of the congregation of Israel (cf. Leviticus 16:15). Thus the idea here conveyed is related to public worship.

The instructions found in this chapter were intended to preserve the moral purity of the people by separating them from the idolatrous religious practices of the nations around them. He speaks of three issues here. In verses two through nine the Israelites were instructed that they were to offer no sacrifices to any other gods. *"And they shall no more offer their sacrifices unto devils, after whom they have gone a whoring. This shall be a statute forever unto them throughout their generations."* (Verse 7). Only the true God of Abraham, Isaac, and Jacob was to be the object of their collective worship. Jehovah alone was to be the object of their focus. This admonition was repeated in Leviticus 20:1- 6.

In Leviticus 17:8-9 they were instructed that all sacrifices were to be offered in one place appointed by God. The New Testament application is stated by Paul in Hebrews 10:25. *"Not forsaking the assembling of ourselves together, as the manner of some is; but exhorting one another: and so much the more, as ye see the day approaching."* This was a call to the Hebrews to public worship. In this worship their focus was to be only on God and His Word. We will speak more of this in the concluding chapter.

Secondly, there was a clear prohibition against the eating of blood (Leviticus 17:10-14). The reason given for this prohibition is that *"the life of the flesh is in the blood."* This issue was covered by earlier ordinances relating to the sacrifices. But what about animals killed simply to eat and not for offering as a sacrifice? For that which was taken by hunting, they were instructed that under no circumstances was the blood to be eaten.

Further, the blood was not to be eaten because *"I have given it to you upon the altar to make an atonement for your souls: for it is the blood that maketh an atonement for the soul"* (vs. 11). We are here reminded that *"the wages of sin is death; but the gift of God is eternal life through Jesus Christ our Lord." (Romans 6:23).* The blood represents life. To offer it upon the altar symbolized the offering of the life. Here, again, we see the "exchange of life" principle alluded to. This emphasis is well stated by Paul in Hebrews 9:22 where he wrote: *"And almost all things are by the law purged with blood; and without the shedding of blood is no remission."* Our positional sanctification is secured by the blood shed by Christ on our behalf at Calvary. It was His life poured out for ours. Because the life is in the blood it is sacred to God. God created life and it returns to Him. Therefore God instructed that no blood was to be eaten. Our worship is to demonstrate the sacredness of life.

The last two verses of chapter seventeen speak of the third important issue as it relates to ecclesiastical sanctification. All food that was to be eaten was to be offered unto God in thanksgiving. In our practice today this is done as we thank Him before each meal for the food we are about to eat. In the Old Testament economy, a clean animal fit for food which died of itself or was killed by another animal could not be offered and thus should not be eaten. If they ate it anyway they became unclean (cf. Exodus 22:31; Leviticus 7:24).

This has an application for us today. Jesus said: *"Therefore I say unto you, Take no thought for your life, what ye shall eat, or what ye shall drink; nor yet for your body, what ye shall put on. Is not the life more than meat, and the body than raiment?"* (Matthew 6:25). As believers, we are set apart unto God. We are not to get tangled up in worldly concerns. We are called to *"Seek ye first the kingdom of God, and his righteousness; and all these things shall be added unto you"* (Matthew 6:33).

If they ate that which first had not been offered unto God they were instructed to wash both their clothes and their body. We are constantly tainted by the world. But there is a way of cleansing. Is this not what Jesus said to Peter who, at first, refused to allow Jesus to wash his feet? Jesus told him that if he refused to allow him to wash his feet

Peter had no part in Him. With that Peter responded: *"Not my feet only, but also my hands and my head."* Then Jesus responded: *"He that is washed needeth not save to wash his feet, but is clean every whit: and ye are clean, but not all."* (cf. John 13:8-10). We are not to get tangled in worldly things. But if we do there is a way to get back on track: *"If we confess our sins, he is faithful and just to forgive us our sins, and to cleanse us from all unrighteousness"* (I John 1:9). By this our fellowship with God is restored. We are also cleansed by His word. Jesus said: *"Now are ye clean through the word which I have spoken unto you."* (John 15:3). Paul wrote: *"Christ also loved the church, and gave himself for it; that he might sanctify and cleanse it with the washing of water by the word."* (Ephesians 5:25b-26). Cleansing also comes to the believer through the daily reading and the absorbing of the living water of God's word. As we approach public worship, we are to come to it with our sins confessed cleansed by His word.

So, in the area of ecclesiastical sanctification we are to order our life in such a manner that we maintain separation from all that is not true worship of the true God. We will have more to say on this issue in the final chapter of this book as we specifically discuss the place of public worship in the life of the believer.

Personal Sanctification

Leviticus Chapters eighteen through twenty discuss the issue of moral purity. This passage begins with a preface (18:1-5), and ends with a clear conclusion in chapter 20, verses 22-26. Chapter eighteen addresses the laws of chastity. Chapter nineteen instructs us in the laws of holiness. Chapter twenty lays down the penalties that would be imposed for not keeping His laws.

One major issue that would confront Israel when they got to the Promised Land was the conflict between two ways of life: one godly, the other ungodly. Archeology has clearly established the evidence showing how totally immoral and degraded were the lifestyles of the Canaanites. God was now preparing the Israelites to withstand the pressures of that coming conflict.

Notice that God prefaces the laws He is about to lay down with a statement of His sovereignty. He states: *"I am the Lord your God."* I am

Jehovah, the Creator and Ruler of all. Because God is absolute holiness, right conduct results when one follows, by God's power and grace, His righteous precepts. The fact that God is holy and, in His holiness He redeemed us, we have the motive we need to order our life to serve and honor Him. In His holiness we may know that He has nothing but our best interest in His heart. Verse three gives three basic prohibitions. They were not to live and act as the Egyptians from whom they were delivered. They were not to live and act like the Canaanites among whom they would find themselves. And they were not to do after their ordinances. Thus they were not only to avoid their evil practices but also their evil principles which were the basis of their evil practices.

The essence of these three chapters is to teach us that we are not to live as the world lives. Peter describes the believing church as *"A chosen generation, a royal priesthood, a holy nation, a peculiar people; that ye should show forth the praises of him who hath called you out of darkness into his marvelous light: which in times past were not a people, but are now the people of God: which had not obtained mercy, but now have obtained mercy."* (I Peter 2:9- 10). How did we become this royal priesthood? Paul explains it to us in Titus 2:14. *"Jesus Christ; who gave himself for us, that he might redeem us from all iniquity, and purify unto himself a peculiar people, zealous of good works."*

The rest of chapter eighteen deals with things related to marriage relationships. The laws laid down here call for the purity of our marriage and sexual relationships. Chapter nineteen is an expansion of the Ten Commandments. Again, we need to be reminded that we are not under the law but under Grace. Yet the moral laws God laid down to the Israelites, establish for us the moral character of God. They demonstrate His holiness. In the Old Testament economy they were to keep the law for fear of judgment. In the New Testament economy we are to live righteously because we love God and His dear Son, our Saviour. It was Jesus who said: *"If ye love me, keep my commandments. He that hath my commandments and keepeth them, he it is that loveth me. If a man love me he will keep my words."* (John 14:15, 21, 23).

Personal sanctification speaks of our responsibility to live righteously in our daily walk. The purpose of the law is to help us understand the difference between that which is clean and that which is unclean (Leviticus 20:24, 25).

These three chapters conclude with the appropriate statement found in verse twenty-six: *"And ye shall be holy unto me: for I am the LORD and am holy, and severed you from other people, that ye should be mine."*

Lessons to be learned

From this chapter of our study we need to learn to be careful how we live, avoiding even the appearance of evil. We must see that the family is to be the heart of all our moral-ethical relationships. We also should now recognize that we are to maintain purity in every avenue of our life. Let us again be reminded that if we have implemented all of the previous principles of worship that are here laid out for us it is possible to step up to this new level because through the previous principles God gives us the enablement.

The Eleventh Principle of Worship

Careful separation (sanctification) from every known aspect of sin is essential for maintaining an intimate relationship with God.

CHAPTER 13

THE PLACE OF DIVINE DISCIPLINE

LEVITICUS 26

No one likes discipline especially when it is applied to them. Yet, the end result of all that we have learned in this study and the principles of worship that have been shared have their culmination in the fact of divine discipline. When we compare the benefits that accrue to the sanctified believer against the cost to us when our fellowship with God is broken by our sin, known or unknown at the time it was committed, God's discipline is seen as an act of His loving grace because its goal is our restoration. This is the clear truth taught in Hebrews 12:5-11. God's chastening is an act of His love (v. 6) and is done for our profit. Note verse 10: *but he* (God) *for our own profit, that we might be partakers of his holiness."* Divine chastening is not punishment. If it was, then God lied to us because He told us that Jesus took all of the punishment due us, past, present and future, upon Himself at the cross. Thus chastening should be viewed as evidence of the new birth, our new relationship with our Creator, and understood as child training. Is that not, after all, what true worship is all about? So we shall see that this final principle of worship simply ties it all together.

A Proper Attitude and its Rewards

In Leviticus 26:1-13 God instructs us about a proper attitude and its rewards. Verses one and two speak of the proper attitude. First, God is to be our primary focus. Why? *"For I am the LORD your God."* He is the holy, loving, caring Creator of the universe. He is all knowing. Thus He knows what is best for us at any moment.

Secondly, He states: *"Ye shall keep my Sabbaths, and reverence my sanctuary."* The observance of the Sabbath was one of the marks that set Israel apart from the heathen. It was a constant reminder to Israel of the creation of the earth encouraging them that their faith was placed in the only one and true God. The word "Sabbath" literally means to desist, cease, or rest and was instituted at creation. *"And on the seventh day God ended his work which he had made; and he rested on the seventh day from all his work which he had made. And God blessed the seventh day, and sanctified it: because that in it he had rested from all his work which God created and made."* (Genesis 2:2-3). The word that is here twice translated "rested" is *shabath* which is the root word for *shabbath* which is translated "sabbath". It simply designated a day of rest, any day. It wasn't until Israel was in the wilderness daily collecting manna that God specified the seventh day as the Sabbath. In Exodus 16:16-22 God instructed them to collect for five days only what they could eat in one day. Then on the sixth day they were to collect enough for two days. Verse 23 recorded God's reason: *"And he said unto them, this is that which the LORD hath said, Tomorrow is the rest of the holy sabbath unto the LORD."* The Sabbath principle is that God said man is to do his work in six days and rest for one (cf. Exodus 16:26-30; 20:8-11). There is no specifying of which day of the calendar week is to be the Sabbath.

In Exodus 31:12-17 the Sabbath, as a special holy (ceremonial) day, was established in the Mosaic Covenant to be unique to Israel. Of the keeping of the Sabbath as a special day God said: *"Wherefore the children of Israel shall keep the Sabbath, to observe the Sabbath throughout their generations, for a perpetual covenant. It is a sign between me and the children of Israel for ever."* (Exodus 31:17) (cf. Ezekiel 20:12). It is an interesting fact that God Himself informed Israel that a day would come when He would cause even the Sabbath as a ceremonial law to cease (cf. Hosea 2:11).

In the Church Age the principle established by the Sabbath ordinance distinguishes the true believer, who sets aside one day of the week to rest and publically worship the true God, from those who profess but are not truly born again and from the rest of the world around them. The true believer is hungry for the teaching of His word and for the unique fellowship experienced in public worship. Again, we see that even in public matters God is to be our primary focus.

"And reverence my sanctuary" is an interesting phrase with a dual meaning. The sanctuary in the Old Testament economy was God's dwelling place in the midst of His people. To reverence the sanctuary was to reverence God. For the believer in the church age the sanctuary reflects two things. God dwells in the true church which is not a building. As He dwells in us, believers who come together in groups for the purpose of collective worship are the church. The building which so many errantly call the church is simply the place where the church congregates.

As true believers are the church our fellow believers should be shown reverence and respect. In John 15:12 Jesus commanded us: *"that ye love one another, as I have loved you."* Remember, His love is unconditional. Therefore we should love one another unconditionally. Paul stated it this way: *"Let nothing be done through strife or vainglory; but in lowliness of mind let each esteem others better than themselves."* (Philippians 2:3). If this biblical principle were followed by believers in their fellowships the only time a church would split would be over doctrinal issues.

This phrase also reminds us that, as God's Spirit indwells us, we are to reverence our own body as the sanctuary of the living God. Thus we are called to keep it from any defilement or carnal sin (cf. I Corinthians 6:19-20). We are again reminded that God has given us a new nature and written His law in our heart (cf. Hebrews 8:10).

So we are to have a proper attitude toward God. He is to be the primary focus of our life. We are to have a proper attitude toward God's sanctuary, our body. As He indwells the true believer we are to love them unconditionally holding them up as better than ourselves. As God through His Spirit indwells us we are called to reverence our own bodies, doing nothing to it or with it that would dishonor the God who indwells us.

The teaching of verses three to ten is simply that rewards (blessings) accrue to those who, with a right attitude, faithfully serve and honor the only one and true God. However, we must understand that God is a debtor to no man. Living righteously has its rewards. We are privileged to live in the presence of our loving God. It was David who wrote: *"In thy presence is fullness of Joy; at thy right hand there are pleasures for evermore."* (Psalm 16:11). As we come to understand it is our privilege to serve and honor the living God, there is a joy that permeates our lives. This occurs because we have come to know from experience as well as from the exercise of our faith that in His unconditional love He only has our best interest at heart.

All of this is keyed to our walking with Him in sweet fellowship. *"And I will set my tabernacle* (His dwelling) *among you: and my soul shall not abhor you. And I will walk among you, and will be your God, and ye shall be my people."* (Leviticus 26:11-12). This same God who broke the bands of the Egyptian bondage and delivered them into freedom promised to enable them to *"go upright."* Everything is by God's grace. Our responsibility is to accept it and allow Him to accomplish His work in us.

A Sober Warning

Verses 14 through 39 give us a sober warning. We are reminded of what causes us to miss out on the very real blessings. We have a tendency not to listen when God speaks. But it is more than not listening. Often, for whatever the reason, we do not pay attention. We do not take the time to do what is necessary to put ourselves in the place where God can speak to us. Remember, praying is when we talk with God. It is through our daily and consistent reading of His word that He speaks to us. When we do not take the time to involve ourselves in these two simple practices, before we know it, we have again slipped into the driver's seat of our lives. Then it becomes so easy for us to think that we know what is best. But this only creates problems for us as it becomes the means of our stepping away from God and thus breaking the fellowship with Him which, in reality, is everything. Refusing to listen leads to rebellion, the resisting of His will. And rebellion leads to Divine discipline. Divine discipline is the way God uses to once again get our attention. The sooner we listen the sooner we find ourselves back in fellowship with Him and in the place of His blessings. That is the wonderful message of God's grace in verses forty through forty-five of this chapter.

This is precisely what Paul was writing about in Hebrews 12:5 and following. *"My son, despise not the chastening of the LORD, nor faint when thou art rebuked of him: for whom the Lord loveth he chasteneth, and scourgeth every son whom he receiveth....But if ye be without chastisement, whereof all are partakers, then ye are bastards, and not sons. Furthermore, we have had fathers of our flesh which corrected us.....For they verily for a few days chastened us after their own pleasure; but he for our profit, that we might be partakers of his holiness. Now no chastening for the present seemeth to be joyous, but grievous: nevertheless, afterward it yieldeth the peaceable fruit of righteousness unto them which are exercise thereby."*

Lessons to Be Learned

Careful obedience brings blessings, both material and spiritual. Disobedience brings Divine discipline tempered by God's grace, the purpose of which is to bring us back into fellowship with Him. Remember, our relationship was fixed at the new birth. Fellowship is linked to obedience. Complete and consistent obedience brings us the joy of intimate fellowship with our Creator.

How I love these words penned by David: *"In thy presence is fullness of joy."* (Psalm 16:11). How often I am reminded that joy and happiness are two different concepts. Happiness is determined by outward circumstances. So I may not always be happy. But joy is determined by an inward and upward relationship and fellowship with our Creator. As long as we, by His grace, maintain that fellowship we will have an overflowing joy.

The Twelfth Principle of Worship

Now we can understand that Divine discipline is not a bad thing. It is not the outpouring of His wrath or judgment upon us. It is the very opposite. It is the outpouring of His love and grace to draw us back into that right relationship with Him that results in overflowing blessings. Thus the twelfth principle of worship is that Divine discipline is administered not to punish but to bring us back into a proper relationship with Him so that we can worship Him as we aught and be blessed by His love. Let not Divine discipline frighten you. Recognize it for what it is: God's love to draw you back into true fellowship, and the evidence that you are His child.

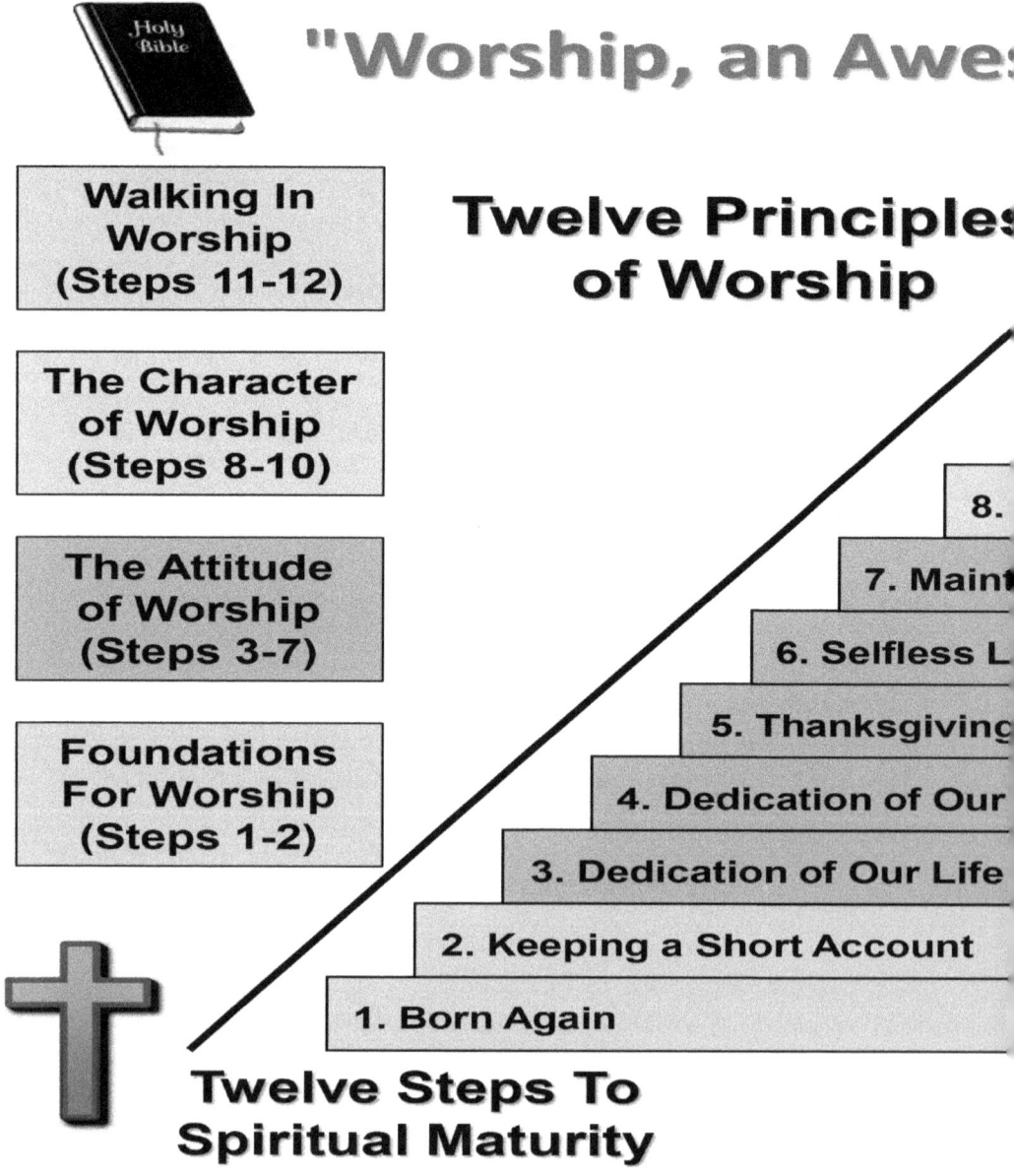

ome Journey of Faith"

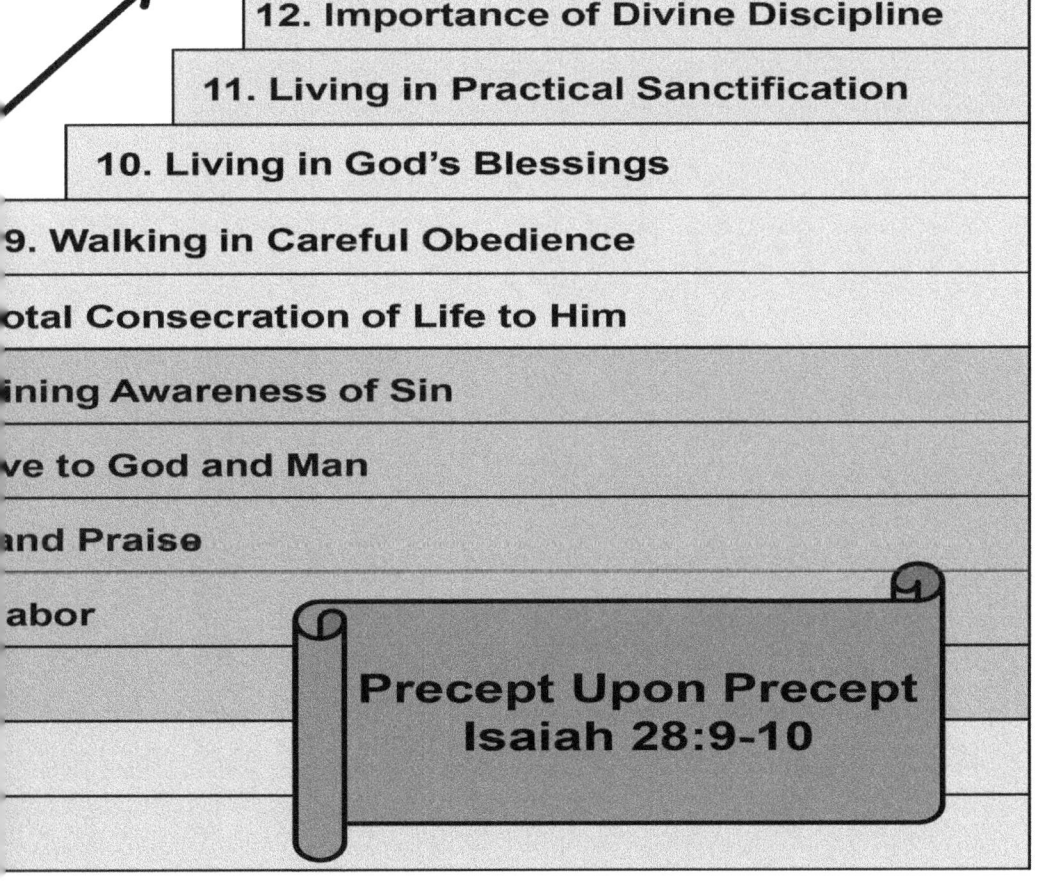

12. Importance of Divine Discipline

11. Living in Practical Sanctification

10. Living in God's Blessings

9. Walking in Careful Obedience

otal Consecration of Life to Him

ining Awareness of Sin

ve to God and Man

and Praise

abor

**Precept Upon Precept
Isaiah 28:9-10**

CHAPTER 14

THE ACT OF PUBLIC WORSHIP

LEVITICUS CHAPTERS 23, 24, 25, 27

As we close this study on worship we must address the issues related to our walk and public worship. We have given much time and space dealing with the issues related to personal worship. We defined worship simply as the believer living in God's presence. This was David's definition of worship as we saw in Psalm 23:6 where he wrote: *"Surely goodness and mercy shall follow me all the days of my life: and I will dwell in the house of the LORD forever."* Worship is living in His presence!

David also shared with us the benefits of living in His presence. In Psalm 16:11 David wrote: *"Thou wilt show me the path of life: in thy presence is fullness of joy; at thy right hand there are pleasures for evermore."* In His presence we discover His will (plan) for our life. Living in His presence (following His plan) results in overflowing joy and brings pleasure that has no end. Truly this makes worship an awesome journey of faith.

Let us now turn our attention to the role of public worship in the life of the believer.

Public Worship Commanded

God's command for His people to participate in public worship in Leviticus, for the most part, is implied. It is implied by God's command to build the Tabernacle and by the establishment of all the feasts, festivals, sacrifices and offerings in which His people were commanded to participate. Eight times in Leviticus 23 the term *convocation* is used. This word denotes a public meeting. About these "convocations" Edward Drew wrote: "The peculiar thing about the word 'feast' in a number of cases where it is repeated in this chapter, is that it is the Hebrew word which means 'to keep an appointment.' It does not have in it the idea of getting together to have an enjoyable time. The Lord really said to Moses, 'These are my appointments with the people. These are the times that I have given you, special times when I will meet with you, and you will come and meet with me.'"[xvi] In the levitical system God made appointments with His people to meet them at certain times, bringing certain offerings and observing the day according to His command. Meeting with God in public convocations was indeed commanded in Leviticus.

In Deuteronomy chapter twelve five times Israel was instructed to worship in a *"place which the LORD thy God hath chosen."* (vv. 5, 11, 14, 18, 21). As Moses is reciting God's commands that were more specifically laid out in Leviticus, it is clear that God directly commanded Israel to publicly worship in a place of His choosing. Public worship was commanded.

In the early church many Jewish believers were considering going back into Rabbinic Judaism, worshipping at the Synagogue, rather than continuing to worship publically with the believers giving cause for Paul to write his Epistle to the Hebrews. In Hebrews 10:19-25 Paul specifically dealt with this issue of neglecting the matter of public worship. Paul warned them against the abandonment of a public profession of their faith. Paul encouraged them to *"Hold fast the profession of our faith without wavering."* They were challenged *"to consider one another to provoke unto love and good works."* He then pointed out that the way to accomplish this was *"not forsaking the assembling of ourselves together."* He went on to challenge them to exhort (encourage) one another. The clear implication is that this is done as believers faithfully gather in public worship, standing together in confidence of faith before the world. Paul does not state the necessity of public worship in terms of a command but as an important practice in our spiritual growth and service. Thus Paul encouraged in the strongest terms that believers should regularly be involved in public worship.

Preparation for Public Worship

One of the great psalms of praise is Psalm 100. This psalm is the ringing conclusion to Psalms 95 through 99. Consider the psalm: *"Make a joyful noise unto the LORD, all ye lands. Serve the LORD with gladness: come before His presence with singing. Know ye that the LORD he is God: it is he that hath made us, and not we ourselves; we are his people, and the sheep of his pasture. Enter into his gates with thanksgiving, and into his courts with praise: be thankful unto him, and bless his name. For the LORD is good; his mercy is everlasting; and his truth endureth to all generations."*

Psalms 95 through 100 are a call to worship. In them we are reminded of what we must do to prepare ourselves for public worship. First, we are to come with a proper attitude. The psalmist instructed: *"O come let us worship and bow down: let us kneel before the LORD our maker."* (Psalm 95:6). Our's should be an attitude of humility and awe. We are to recognize Him for who He is, the Creator God, and see ourselves in relation to Him as His creation. We are to honor and pay Him homage as we publically worship. We are to come with an attitude of praise for His Name. *"Let them praise thy great and terrible name; for it is holy....Exalt ye the LORD our God, and worship at his footstool; for he is holy."* (Psalm 99:3, 5).

If we are to truly experience the blessings of public worship it is not only important to recognize who God is and who we are in relation to Him. We need also to come with a joyful heart. The thought is expressed over and over in these six psalms. Three of the psalms begin with the call to: *"Sing unto the LORD."* Psalm 97 uses the terms "rejoice" and "be glad." Psalm 99 speaks of "praise" for His holy name. Psalm 100 encourages us to *"make a joyful noise"* and come into His presence with singing. When our heart is right we will even recognize that the offering provides an opportunity to express our joy. Paul stated: *Every man according as he purposes in his heart, so let him give; not grudgingly, or of necessity: for God loveth a cheerful giver."* (II Cor. 9:7). The Greek word translated "cheerful" is *hilaros* from which we get our word hilarious. If we come with a joyful heart we will give with a merry heart. Even the opportunity to give offers a way to express a joyful and thankful heart. If we are to truly worship Him in the public setting we need to come with a joyful heart.

Over the years I have had many opportunities to lead congregational singing. If you look at people's faces it appears that most sing as though their stomach hurts. Surely if our heart is prepared even the singing of the hymns gives opportunity for us to both express the joy of our heart and show it in the expressions of our faces. I am always moved when the choir sings and I see one or more in the choir expressing on their faces the joy of the song they are singing. This is just one way that we exhort and encourage one another through public worship.

One of the most difficult things for us to do is to lay aside all the stress and worries of the day. Yet, if we would just order our schedule so that we could spend some quiet time, just a few short minutes, in prayer and in the Word before we leave to meet with the church in worship, God could calm and prepare our hearts to enter into His presence joyfully. It is a matter of preparing and resting our life and circumstances in His hands. Remember, we are meeting with our Lord! Let us prepare to come with a joyful heart.

Thirdly, we are to come to public worship with a thankful heart (Psalm 100:4). Many years ago someone suggested a great way to develop a consistently thankful heart. As you read your Bible each day write down every promise you find. At the end of the week, pick one, memorize the verse, and begin claiming that promise. At the end of the first month you will be claiming three promises. At the end of the first year you will be claiming 51 promises. It is not long before you discover how faithful God is. That is enough cause for a thankful heart. You also will have memorized at least 51 Scripture verses. And that is a blessing as God has promised to bless those who fill their heart and mind with His word. We are to come with a thankful heart.

Fourth, we need to come with an expectant heart. The psalmist said: *"Today if ye will hear his voice, harden not your hearts."* (Psalm

95:7b, 8a). Because so many come to public worship unprepared they simply tolerate the service and the sermon (God's message). They come to the service out of a sense of obligation. Many come to public worship unprepared or for the wrong reason. Because they are unprepared they can hardly wait for the preacher to quit and for the service to end.

God speaks to us through His Word. First, He cleanses us through His spoken word. Jesus told His disciples: *"Now ye are clean through the word which I have spoken unto you."* (John 15:3). Paul put it this way: *"that he might sanctify and cleanse it (the church) with the washing of water by the word."* (Eph. 5:26). Some years ago when I was a young pastor one of our men whom I had led to the Lord and discipled into the church fellowship came to me after a service and thanked me for preaching a hard sermon that morning. He told me that the Lord showed him through the message that he had some things in his life that he needed, with God's help, to work on. Those experiences, for most pastors, are the exception rather than the rule. But if the worshipper's heart is right he will understand that sometimes God chastens and reminds us that we need to commit some things to Him to clean up in our lives. This is part of the process of "exhorting and provoking one another unto good works."

Through the preaching of the Word we should be encouraged and strengthened in our resolve to remain faithful to the Lord in our life and service. Most good sermons do three things: exhort, provoke and encourage. We need to come with an expectant heart. When we meet with God and His people in public worship we should never go from that meeting the same people who came. Surely, just to meet with God should affect in some way our life. We need to come prepared to worship.

The Purpose of Public Worship

If we are to understand the purpose of public worship we must first understand the focus of our worship. In His temptations, Jesus was asked by Satan to worship him. But Jesus answered: *"Thou shalt worship the Lord they God, and him only shalt thou serve.* (Luke 4:8). In the 16th Psalm at least four times David expressed that his focus was the Lord. Jesus counseled: *"Seek ye first the kingdom of God and his righteousness."*

(Matt. 6:33a). Our focus should not be on the pastor, the choir, the music. Our focus must be only on our precious Lord. We are in the service to meet with Him.

That is our primary purpose. We are there to honor and glorify Him and Him alone. This is the purpose wherein we are blessed.

It is also the purpose of public worship to give us opportunity to encourage and strengthen one another. Our faith is strengthened as we recognize that we are not alone in our quest to honor and serve our risen Lord. I receive such a lifting of my heart and spirit as I join my voice with others in the choruses of praise and honor to our God. My heart is encouraged as we pray together and thus share one another's burdens. And in all of this my participation is an encouragement to the others who are present.

Thus the purpose of worship involves both giving and receiving. We give to God the glory due Him. In the process we are encouraged and strengthened in our faith walk enabling us to better live a life of worship thus making this awesome journey of faith easier. At the same time, as we joyfully worship, we are encouraging and strengthening those around us.

The Ingredients of Public Worship

There are a number of things that God's word indicates should be a part of the worship process. All ingredients that become a part of the public worship experience should do nothing less than exalt and honor our Lord. Not all ingredients necessarily need to be a part of every public worship experience. Consider some of the ingredients mentioned in Scripture. Music should play an important role, both vocal and instrumental. The Psalms, in particular, are full of references to singing and singers. II Samuel 6:5 gives reference to *"all manner of instruments made of fir wood, even on harps and on psalteries, and on timbrels, and on cornets, and on cymbals."* I Kings 1:40 is a specific reference to the use of wind instruments such as might be the clarinet, etc. Leviticus speaks of the use of trumpets in worship. Timbrels and cymbals are percussion instruments. The purpose of music in the public worship experience is to help the worshippers to focus on the

Lord. Music, vocal or instrumental, that draws attention to itself or to the worldly has no place in public worship.

Prayer should have a primary role as prayer is man's way of communicating with the Lord. Again, the focus of prayer should be on the Lord. The Scripture admonishes us to pray according to His will. Prayer should embody that which we know to be compatible to the very character of God. To pray in Jesus' name is to indicate that we are confident our prayer is compatible to His will. Public prayer should be offered from a heart that is in tune with the Lord and yet encompasses the needs and concerns of the congregation. We are commanded to *"come boldly unto the throne of grace, that we may obtain mercy, and find grace to help in time of need."* (Hebrews 4:16).

Thanksgiving is a major theme both in the Psalms and in the writings of Paul and others in the New Testament. Praise and thanksgiving generally go together and are important ingredients in the public worship experience.

Praise and thanksgiving are offered in so many ways including the sharing of testimonies of God's faithfulness.

Three times it is recorded that God stated: *"And none shall appear before me empty."* (Exodus 23:15; 34:20; Deuteronomy 16:16). In each instance the worshipper was to bring a gift that was to be offered unto the Lord. If we today were to follow the Mosaic code we would discover that they were required to give far beyond the tenth by the time they offered all of the required sacrifices (cf. Numbers 29:39). Most are unaware that in the Mosaic economy three tithes were required. There was the tithe that was given unto the LORD through the Tabernacle (Leviticus 27:26-34). The second tithe was given to the Levites who had received no agricultural land (Numbers 18:20-21). The Levites then were required to tithe that which was given them (Numbers 18:25-29). The third required tithe is recorded in Deuteronomy 14:28-29. This was a special tithe collected every third year and was to be distributed *"to the Levite, and the stranger, and the fatherless, and the widow."* Essentially this tithe was to be distributed to the poor. Note this was not a government program. It was administered locally by the head of each household (cf. Deuteronomy 26:12-14).

In the New Testament economy the believers are to give as God prospers them. Nowhere, either in the Old or New Testaments, is there any suggestion that the tithe was removed as the basic standard for giving. Remember, tithes were given to God by Abraham long before the law commanded them. Financial stewardship is an important ingredient in the believer's public worship experience and needs to be seen as an act of honoring our God who has given us everything. As we saw earlier, the worshipper is to give hilariously.

The final key element to consider is found in words of instruction given to Timothy. Paul exhorted him to: *"Preach the word; be instant in season, and out of season; reprove, rebuke exhort with all longsuffering and doctrine."* (I Timothy 4:2). Preaching was an integral part of the early church activity beginning shortly after Pentecost. Paul, in I Cor. 1:21 stated: *"For after that in the wisdom of God the world by wisdom knew not God, it pleased God by the foolishness of preaching to save them that believe."* Preaching is to be based upon God's Word, teaching the Word for the purpose that the lost may be convicted of their need to be saved, and that the saved may come to understand how to better live in God's presence and become aware of the resources He makes available to all who will believe.

Paul clearly stated the purpose of teaching/preaching the scriptures in II Timothy 3:16, 17 where he stated: *"All scripture is given by inspiration of God, and is profitable for doctrine, for reproof, for correction, for instruction in righteousness: that the man of God may be perfect, thoroughly furnished unto all good works."* Preaching should lead the lost to salvation. It should play a major role in helping the believer to grow and mature in his faith and walk. Thus it should play a central role in the believer's public worship experience. It is through the preaching of the Word that God speaks to the heart of both the unbeliever and the believer if they come with a receptive (prepared) heart.

But let us remember that preaching must be the sharing of God's Word. Jesus warned: *"Howbeit in vain do they worship me, teaching for doctrines the commandments of men."* (Mark 7:7). Carry your Bible. Follow along to be sure you are sitting under a man who is faithfully teaching the Word. If he is preaching the Word you are blessed. If he is not you need to find another who is.

If we thus understand the role of preaching from this biblical perspective, as we enter into that part of the activity of public worship, we will need to prayerfully ask God to speak to us through the message. Perhaps if we did that we would no longer find cause to criticize the sermon. In every sermon we can find something that speaks to our needs, to our heart, if we just listen with a seeking and receptive heart. Then we will go from the public worship experience saying that it was good to be in the Lord's house with His people.

The Results of Public Worship

Public worship results in the believer being encouraged and strengthened in his awesome journey of faith. He is blessed because he met with the Lord and with the Lord's people. If all of the twelve principles of worship we have learned in this study are being applied in your life, public worship will result in a joy and peace that we cannot fully realize in any other way. Yes, worship is an awesome journey of faith that necessarily includes the regular participation in public worship which completes the whole equation. Remember, *"For where two or three are gathered together in my name, there am I in the midst of them."* (Matt. 18:20).

A Closing Thought

Notice the closing verse of the book of Leviticus. *"These are the commandments which the LORD commanded Moses for the children of Israel in Mount Sinai."* (Leviticus 27:34). This book was written for the instruction of worshippers. This closing verse impressively declares that worship consists not merely in prayer, praise, and public ceremonies, but in such a complete consecration to God that over person and property alike can be placed this inscription: "Holiness unto the LORD."

Go forth and enjoy worship. Walk and live in HIS presence! Worship is indeed an awesome journey of faith!

ENDNOTES

[i] Harper's Bible Dictionary. Harper & Brothers, New York, NY. 1952, pg. III

[ii] Pictorial Bible Dictionary. Zondervan, Grand Rapids, MI 1963. Pg III

[iii] Goldberg, Louis, LEVITICUS. Zondervan. Grand Rapids, MI 1980. Pg IV

[iv] Harper's Bible Dictionary. Harper & Brothers, NY, NY; 1954. Pg 2

[v] Drew, Edward, Studies in the book of Leviticus. Lont & Overkamp Pub. Co. Patterson, NJ 1937. Pg 6

[vi] Tenney, Merrill C., The Zondervan Pictoral Bible Dictionary, Zondervan Publishing Co. Grand Rapids, MI. 1963; pg 13

[vii] Ibid

[viii] Bonar, Andrew, A., Commentary on Leviticus, The Banner of Truth Trust. Carlisle, PA. 1983; pg 28

[ix] Ibid; pg 29

[x] Ibid; pg 33

[xi] Erdman, Charles R., The book of Leviticus, Baker Book House, Grand Rapids, MI. 1951: pg 45

[xii] Bonar, Andrew A., Commentary on Leviticus, The Banner of Truth Trust. Carlisle, PA. 1983; pg 45

[xiii] Erdman, Charles R., The book of Leviticus, Baker Book House, Grand Rapids, MI. 1951; pg 50

[xiv] Atkinson, Basil F. C., The Pocket Commentary of the Bible; Leviticus, Richard Clay & Co., London, England; pg 54

[xv] Nicoll, W. Robertson Ed., The Expositor's Greek Testament, Volume III; Wm. B. Eerdmans Publishing Co, Grand Rapids, MI. 1961; pg 68

[xvi] Drew, Edward, Studies in the book of Leviticus. Lont & Overcamp Pub. Co. Patterson, NJ 1937; pg. 83

BIBLIOGRAPHY

≤≥

Atkinson, Basil F. C., *The Pocket Commentary of the Bible: Leviticus.* London, W.C.: Henry E. Walter LTD.

Bonar, Andrew A., *A Commentary on Leviticus.* Carlisle, PA: The Banner of Truth Trust, 1983

Drew, Edward, *Studies in the Book of Leviticus.* Patterson, NJ: Lont & Overkamp Publishing Co., 1937

Erdman, Charles R., *The Book of Leviticus.* Grand Rapids: Baker Book House, 1951

Gibbs, Alfred P., *Worship, The Christian's Highest Occupation.* Kansas City: Walterick Publishers

Goldberg, Louis, *Leviticus.* Grand Rapids: Zondervan Publishing House, 1980

Green, Oliver B., *The Epistle of Paul the Apostle to the Hebrews.* Greenville: The Gospel Hour, Inc. 1965

Henry, Matthew, *Commentary on the Whole Bible.* Grand Rapids: Zondervan Publishing House, 1961

Pink, Arthur W., *An Exposition of Hebrews.* Grand Rapids: Baker Book House, 1963